ROGER WILLIAMS AND THE MASSACHUSETTS MAGISTRATES

Problems in American Civilization

UNDER THE EDITORIAL DIRECTION OF *George Rogers Taylor*

Puritanism in Early America
Roger Williams and the Massachusetts Magistrates
The Causes of the American Revolution, *Revised*
Benjamin Franklin and the American Character
The Declaration of Independence and the Constitution, *Revised*
Hamilton and the National Debt
The Turner Thesis concerning the Role of the Frontier in American History, *Revised*
The War of 1812—Past Justifications and Present Interpretations
The Great Tariff Debate, 1820–1830
The Meaning of Jacksonian Democracy
The Removal of the Cherokee Nation—Manifest Destiny or National Dishonor?
Jackson versus Biddle—The Struggle over the Second Bank of the United States
The Transcendentalist Revolt against Materialism
The Compromise of 1850
The Causes of the American Civil War
Slavery as a Cause of the Civil War, *Revised*
Lincoln and the Coming of the Civil War
The Americanness of Walt Whitman
Reconstruction in the South
Mark Twain's *Huckleberry Finn*
Democracy and the Gospel of Wealth
John D. Rockefeller—Robber Baron or Industrial Statesman?
The Pullman Boycott of 1894—The Problem of Federal Intervention
Booker T. Washington and His Critics—The Problem of Negro Leadership
William Jennings Bryan and the Campaign of 1896
American Imperialism in 1898
Roosevelt, Wilson, and the Trusts
Pragmatism and American Culture
Wilson at Versailles
The Steel Strike of 1919
The New Deal—Revolution or Evolution? *Revised*
Franklin D. Roosevelt and the Supreme Court
American Neutrality and the Spanish Civil War
Pearl Harbor—Roosevelt and the Coming of the War
The Yalta Conference
Industry-wide Collective Bargaining—Promise or Menace?
Education for Democracy—The Debate over the Report of the President's Commission on Higher Education
Evolution and Religion—The Conflict between Science and Theology in Modern America
Immigration—An American Dilemma
Loyalty in a Democratic State
Desegregation and the Supreme Court

Roger Williams

AND THE MASSACHUSETTS MAGISTRATES

EDITED WITH AN INTRODUCTION BY

Theodore P. Greene
AMHERST COLLEGE

Problems in American Civilization

D. C. HEATH AND COMPANY: Boston

PRINTED IN THE UNITED STATES OF AMERICA

INTRODUCTION

IN October of the year 1635 the civil authorities of the Massachusetts Bay colony with the advice and consent of the ministers of the Massachusetts churches sentenced Roger Williams, minister of the church at Salem, "to depart out of our jurisdiction." With this sentence of banishment the Massachusetts magistrates hoped they had provided a final answer to all those vexing questions which Roger Williams had raised among them during the previous four years.

The case of the Massachusetts magistrates versus Roger Williams would not, however, come to any easy conclusion. Within ten years a notable series of publications in England brought the whole affair to the judgment of a wider audience. In a sequence of six letters and books published during the years from 1643 to 1652 John Cotton, as spokesman for the Massachusetts authorities, debated with Roger Williams the justice of the original sentence, the true nature of the church, and the proper meaning of religious liberty. These writings did not limit themselves to simple repetition of the original controversy. During his years of exile in the wilderness of Rhode Island Roger Williams had come to see the importance of religious liberty in ways which he had only dimly sensed while a young minister at Salem. John Cotton too had developed a more careful rationale for the banishment of this troublemaker than the magistrates themselves had felt necessary in 1635. Both Williams and Cotton, then, drew upon subsequent reflection and experience in their accounts of the original controversy. But another weighty consideration also influenced their writings. At the time of publication England was in the midst of those civil wars often known as the Puritan Revolution. Questions of the proper relations of church and state, the desirable extent of religious toleration, and the true nature of the church were vital and fighting matters in the mother country. In reviving the old controversy between Williams and the Massachusetts magistrates both authors aimed to influence present decisions as well as to justify past ones. How the world understood the significance of this case, both men knew, might shape the future as well as determine a verdict upon the past.

In the three hundred and more years since Cotton and Williams debated with each other, any final verdict on this case has remained difficult to achieve. Again and again historians have passed judgment in favor of Williams or of the Massachusetts court—only to be rebutted by subsequent scholars. In the process, however, new dimensions have repeatedly been added to our understanding of the issues in this controversy. Writers have drawn upon later perspectives, upon greater experience with religious liberty or with democracy, upon more extensive historical scholarship, to see aspects of the original controversy which had been neglected. Like Williams and Cotton in the 1640's, men have also used their analyses of this past event to promote present policies and attitudes. Though they have differed on many conclusions, all have agreed that the case of Roger Williams raised questions of fundamental and continuing importance.

To determine what those questions were, to decide what was the true significance of the controversy between

Roger Williams and the Massachusetts authorities is the problem raised by these readings.

The selections included here range through four centuries. From the seventeenth century come the relevant contemporary entries from *Winthrop's Journal* and portions of the subsequent debate between Williams and Cotton. From the early eighteenth century is taken Cotton Mather's spirited dismissal of the "turbulent and singular opinions" of Williams. Two nineteenth-century denominational historians then present sharply contrasting but essentially simple interpretations of the controversy. For the Baptist Knowles it was clearly and solely a matter of liberty of conscience—a concept which the Puritans were too medieval to understand. For the Congregationalist Dexter it was almost exclusively a matter of political "subversion"—Williams threatened to bring upon the society external attack and internal chaos.

Five lengthy selections from twentieth-century writers conclude the book and demonstrate that Roger Williams has attracted more serious attention among recent generations than at any time since his banishment. Men like Parrington and Brockunier discovered in Williams the first modern American, the first great hero of the American democratic tradition. Apparently regarding religion as irrelevant except for its social implications, these "Progressive historians" saw the old controversy as essentially one over political and social philosophies. In Parrington's eyes the concern of Williams for "religious toleration was only a necessary deduction from the major principles of his political theory." To Brockunier "the Salem rebellion was in substance a demand for the right of setting up a democratic opposition to those who had obtained power." If previous historians had largely neglected the democratic dimensions of this conflict, these writers more than redressed the balance.

Within the last decade historians have reacted against this tendency to picture Williams as essentially a modern secular liberal motivated by concerns similar to those which animated the Progressive Movement and the New Deal. Perry Miller, in a remarkably fresh analysis of Williams's own writings, attempted "to cut through the fog of adulation to the much greater—although often more puzzling—human being who founded Providence and who fought the fight for freedom by his own lights and not by anybody else's." More thoroughly versed in Puritan thought than their predecessors, scholars like Miller, Edmund Morgan, and Alan Simpson have tried to set the old controversy of the 1630's more accurately within the intellectual context of that day. These final three writers emphasize that it was not a struggle between modern liberalism and Puritan medievalism. They agree that the dispute arose because Roger Williams was more Puritan than the Massachusetts Puritans, that he shared all the essential concerns of his opponents but feared that any compromises would undermine the integrity of their religious life. These recent writers assert that Williams differed fundamentally from many superficial modern supporters of religious liberty. He did not believe that any religion was as good as any other or as none. He simply felt sure that "forced worship stinks in God's nostrils." He did not wish to separate church and state in order primarily to preserve the peace and purity of the state. He insisted upon separation to maintain the purity and integrity of the church. He opposed linking political and economic privilege to church membership not because of an egalitarian social philosophy but because such extraneous privileges corrupted the honesty of the religious life. Religious liberty, in short, was for Williams not a greater liberty for worldly pursuits but a true liberty from worldly preoccupations.

Though the three final selections agree on this description of Williams's position, important differences of emphasis remain. Edmund Morgan, explaining the dilemma of John Winthrop and the Massachusetts magistrates, portrays the demands of Roger Williams in the 1630's as so utopian and so self-righteous that they threatened the survival of the colony and passed the bounds of responsible morality. Perry Miller at times seems to assert that a principle of literary criticism lay at the heart of the controversy between Williams and Winthrop. Where a prosaic magistrate like Winthrop saw the Old Testament filled with commandments, models, and analogies for the regulation of life in New England, the real peculiarity of Williams, according to Miller, was that he read the Old Testament as a body of metaphors not to be copied slavishly, metaphors or "types" whose meaning was revealed fully only after the coming of Christ. Even if one sees this difference in reading the Old Testament as a symptom rather than the source of the conflict between Winthrop and Williams, Miller provides an important clue here to essential differences of temperament and orientation which played a part in the sentence of banishment. The concluding selection is a chapter from Alan Simpson's study of *Puritanism in Old and New England.* Its historical value is to explain the position of Roger Williams within the context of the whole Puritan movement and to demonstrate how his political views were the product of his religious concern. Its more general value, perhaps, is to demonstrate the fate of Williams's experiment in Rhode Island. Roger Williams had feared the hypocrisy, the loss of purity and vitality within the church which he was sure would be the fruit of the Massachusetts system—and which did in fact overtake that system before it moved toward a more general religious liberty. Simpson concludes, however, that the separation of church and state in Rhode Island did not in itself prove to be any sure guarantee of the integrity and vitality of the religious spirit.

How one views the relevance of this three-hundred-year-old controversy to the problems of modern Americans depends, of course, upon what one sees at stake in 1635 and what one sees as crucial today. For Knowles in the 1830's the answer seemed easy. The principle of liberty of conscience had been the issue in 1635 and had since become a sure, uncomplicated foundation of American religion and welfare. For Brockunier in the 1930's the answer was different but almost equally easy. It is my own view that recent scholarship has now made available a fuller, more accurate, and more complex understanding of the sources of Roger Williams's thought and of the problems he raised for the Massachusetts magistrates. At the same time recent developments in American life have made an understanding of the issues raised in this case more relevant than ever for crucial questions of contemporary American civilization.

The years of the Cold War have forced Americans to face afresh the difficult dilemma of liberty and security. Back in 1630 the Massachusetts authorities had prided themselves upon the autonomy of each congregation and assumed that any differences of opinion could be ironed out through mutual discussion. By 1635, however, they had imposed economic sanctions upon the Salem congregation and banished its minister from the colony. Any violation of their original principles, any loss to the future spiritual and intellectual vitality of their enterprise seem to have weighed little against their fears of interference from abroad and dissension from within. After the Security Act of 1950, the many official investigations, dismissals, and even deportations of recent years, Americans cannot look upon the actions of the Massachusetts magistrates with quite the same easy condescension which characterized some historians of the nineteenth and early twentieth century. If we are honest with ourselves, we cannot fail to give the John Winthrops of 1635 a hearing. If we care about the quality and vitality of our national life, however, we cannot dismiss a Roger Williams simply as a "subversive." To understand fully what was at stake in 1635 may give us a fuller perspective on what is at stake, under different circumstances, when fears for security lead us to curtail liberty today.

Finally the recent Supreme Court decisions and the proposals for federal aid to education have forced all Americans to reconsider the proper relations between church and state. In fact the case of Roger Williams raises this question in a more significant way than the Supreme Court decisions on prayer and Bible reading in the public schools. The Court cases have been argued largely on behalf of atheists or minority religious groups protesting against compulsory exposure to religious exercises of a dominant group. Roger Williams was an ordained minister of the dominant and only religious faith in Massachusetts. He contended that any use of state authority to impose any semblance of religious worship destroyed the integrity of religion and offended God. Those who see the Supreme Court decisions as an attack on all religion have never tried to understand the religious experience as Williams understood it. Those who hail Williams as a prophet of religious liberty but do not take religion seriously also do not understand what Williams felt as the chief reason and source for preserving liberty. If religion were simply a means for inculcating morality, preserving social order, and determining respectability, Williams would probably be glad to make it a function of the state.

Now as in his lifetime an encounter with Roger Williams compels men to think more seriously than they are accustomed to do about the nature of their faith and its social implications.

CONTENTS

The Clash of Issues

I. *What Was the Cause of the Banishment of Roger Williams?*

Whereas the Truth is, his banishment proceeded not against him, or his, for his own refusal of worship, but for seditious opposition against the patent, and against the oath of fidelity offered to the people.

John Cotton, 1644

There is one commodity for the sake of which most of God's children in New England have run their mighty hazards. . . . It is a liberty of searching after God's most holy mind and pleasure.

Out of this most precious and invaluable jewel, if you suffer Satan (that grand thief and cheater) to bereave you, and that it shall be a crime, humbly and peaceably to question even laws and statutes, or what ever is even publicly taught and delivered, you will most certainly find your selves . . . but where you were, enslaved and captivated.

Roger Williams, 1652

We are led to the conclusion, that the cause of Mr. Williams's banishment is to be found in the great principle which has immortalized his name, that THE CIVIL POWER HAS NO JURISDICTION OVER THE CONSCIENCE.

James D. Knowles, 1834

Mr. Williams was mistaken in supposing that the subject of the rights of conscience had anything whatever to do with the action of the Court upon his case; action, in reality, solely taken in view of his seditious, defiant, and pernicious posture toward the State.

Henry M. Dexter, 1876

II. *What Was the Source of Williams's Stand?*

The just renown of Roger Williams has too long been obscured by ecclesiastical historians, who in emphasizing his defense of the principle of toleration have overlooked the fact that religious toleration was only a necessary deduction from the major principles of his political theory. . . . He was primarily a political philosopher rather than a theologian.

Vernon L. Parrington, 1927

Even for theologians in an ultratheological era, the cast of Williams's mind was too much theological: therein consists his challenge to the twentieth century as well as to the seventeenth.

Perry Miller, 1953

The crime of Roger Williams was that he dared to oppose and to appeal to the people . . . here was a man already too suspiciously democratic, too resolutely a believer in the value of untrammeled public discussion.

Samuel H. Brockunier, 1940

bership not because of an egalitarian social philosophy but because such extraneous privileges corrupted the honesty of the religious life. Religious liberty, in short, was for Williams not a greater liberty for worldly pursuits but a true liberty from worldly preoccupations.

Though the three final selections agree on this description of Williams's position, important differences of emphasis remain. Edmund Morgan, explaining the dilemma of John Winthrop and the Massachusetts magistrates, portrays the demands of Roger Williams in the 1630's as so utopian and so self-righteous that they threatened the survival of the colony and passed the bounds of responsible morality. Perry Miller at times seems to assert that a principle of literary criticism lay at the heart of the controversy between Williams and Winthrop. Where a prosaic magistrate like Winthrop saw the Old Testament filled with commandments, models, and analogies for the regulation of life in New England, the real peculiarity of Williams, according to Miller, was that he read the Old Testament as a body of metaphors not to be copied slavishly, metaphors or "types" whose meaning was revealed fully only after the coming of Christ. Even if one sees this difference in reading the Old Testament as a symptom rather than the source of the conflict between Winthrop and Williams, Miller provides an important clue here to essential differences of temperament and orientation which played a part in the sentence of banishment. The concluding selection is a chapter from Alan Simpson's study of *Puritanism in Old and New England.* Its historical value is to explain the position of Roger Williams within the context of the whole Puritan movement and to demonstrate how his political views were the product of his religious concern. Its more general value, perhaps, is to demonstrate the fate of Williams's experiment in Rhode Island. Roger Williams had feared the hypocrisy, the loss of purity and vitality within the church which he was sure would be the fruit of the Massachusetts system—and which did in fact overtake that system before it moved toward a more general religious liberty. Simpson concludes, however, that the separation of church and state in Rhode Island did not in itself prove to be any sure guarantee of the integrity and vitality of the religious spirit.

How one views the relevance of this three-hundred-year-old controversy to the problems of modern Americans depends, of course, upon what one sees at stake in 1635 and what one sees as crucial today. For Knowles in the 1830's the answer seemed easy. The principle of liberty of conscience had been the issue in 1635 and had since become a sure, uncomplicated foundation of American religion and welfare. For Brockunier in the 1930's the answer was different but almost equally easy. It is my own view that recent scholarship has now made available a fuller, more accurate, and more complex understanding of the sources of Roger Williams's thought and of the problems he raised for the Massachusetts magistrates. At the same time recent developments in American life have made an understanding of the issues raised in this case more relevant than ever for crucial questions of contemporary American civilization.

The years of the Cold War have forced Americans to face afresh the difficult dilemma of liberty and security. Back in 1630 the Massachusetts authorities had prided themselves upon the autonomy of each congregation and assumed that any differences of opinion could be ironed out through mutual discussion. By 1635, however, they had imposed economic sanctions upon the Salem congregation and banished its minister from the colony. Any violation of their original principles, any loss to the future spiritual and intellectual vitality of their enterprise seem to have weighed little against their fears of interference from abroad and dissension from within. After the Security Act of 1950, the many official investigations, dismissals, and even deportations of recent years, Americans cannot look upon the actions of the Massachusetts magistrates with quite the same easy condescension which characterized some historians of the nineteenth and early twentieth century. If we are honest with ourselves, we cannot fail to give the John Winthrops of 1635 a hearing. If we care about the quality and vitality of our national life, however, we cannot dismiss a Roger Williams simply as a "subversive." To understand fully what was at stake in 1635 may give us a fuller perspective on what is at stake, under different circumstances, when fears for security lead us to curtail liberty today.

Finally the recent Supreme Court decisions and the proposals for federal aid to education have forced all Americans to reconsider the proper relations between church and state. In fact the case of Roger Williams raises this question in a more significant way than the Supreme Court decisions on prayer and Bible reading in the public schools. The Court cases have been argued largely on behalf of atheists or minority religious groups protesting against compulsory exposure to religious exercises of a dominant group. Roger Williams was an ordained minister of the dominant and only religious faith in Massachusetts. He contended that any use of state authority to impose any semblance of religious worship destroyed the integrity of religion and offended God. Those who see the Supreme Court decisions as an attack on all religion have never tried to understand the religious experience as Williams understood it. Those who hail Williams as a prophet of religious liberty but do not take religion seriously also do not understand what Williams felt as the chief reason and source for preserving liberty. If religion were simply a means for inculcating morality, preserving social order, and determining respectability, Williams would probably be glad to make it a function of the state.

Now as in his lifetime an encounter with Roger Williams compels men to think more seriously than they are accustomed to do about the nature of their faith and its social implications.

In nine-tenths of his opinions Roger Williams saw eye to eye with the Cottons and Winthrops who banished him. . . . Nor did he break with them because he had any quarrel with aristocracy as a principle of political government or any ambition to found a democratic community. He broke with them because he convinced himself, in a series of collisions with the Massachusetts authorities, that they were not taking sufficiently seriously the gulf which separates the regenerate from the unregenerate and that the covenanted community of the New England pattern was actually a horrible perversion of God's declared will.

ALAN SIMPSON, 1955

PART I. HOW THE CONTROVERSY APPEARED TO THREE OF THE ORIGINAL PARTICIPANTS

John Winthrop: Winthrop's Journal

For the basic narrative of the events which culminated in the banishment of Roger Williams from Massachusetts Winthrop's Journal *is the best original source. John Winthrop himself was Governor of the colony during the early stages of the controversy until May, 1634. Although he maintained a personal friendship with Williams throughout his life, Winthrop never approved of the positions which Williams took and never questioned the necessity for removing that impetuous soul from Massachusetts Bay.*

1631

(Jan. 5.) The ship *Lyon,* Mr. William Peirce, master, arrived at Nantasket. She brought Mr. Williams, (a godly minister,) with his wife.

(April 12.) At a court holden at Boston, (upon information to the governor, that they of Salem had called Mr. Williams to the office of a teacher,) a letter was written from the court to Mr. Endecott to this effect: That whereas Mr. Williams had refused to join with the congregation at Boston, because they would not make a public declaration of their repentance for having communion with the churches of England, while they lived there; and, besides, had declared his opinion, that the magistrate might not punish the breach of the Sabbath, nor any other offence, as it was a breach of the first table; therefore, they marvelled they would choose him without advising with the council; and withal desiring him, that they would forbear to proceed till they had conferred about it.

1633

(November.) The ministers in the bay and Sagus did meet, once a fortnight, at one of their houses by course, where some question of moment was debated. Mr. Skelton, the pastor of Salem, and Mr. Williams, who was removed from Plymouth thither, (but not in any office, though he exercised by way of prophecy,) took some exception against it, as fearing it might grow in time to a presbytery or superintendency, to the prejudice of the churches' liberties. But this fear was without cause; for they were all clear in that point, that no church or person can have power over another church; neither did they in their meetings exercise any such jurisdiction, etc.

(Dec. 27.) The governor and assistants met at Boston, and took into consideration a treatise, which Mr. Williams (then of Salem) had sent to them, and which he had formerly written to the governor and council of Plymouth, wherein, among other things, he disputes

From *Winthrop's Journal,* edition in *Original Narratives of Early American History* (New York, 1908), Vol. I, pp. 57, 61–2, 112–13, 116–17, 142, 149, 154, 155, 157, 162, 168.

their right to the lands they possessed here, and concluded that, claiming by the king's grant, they could have no title, nor otherwise, except they compounded with the natives. For this, taking advice with some of the most judicious ministers, (who much condemned Mr. Williams's error and Presumption,) they gave order, that he should be convented at the next court, to be censured, etc. There were three passages chiefly whereat they were much offended: 1, for that he chargeth King James to have told a solemn public lie, because in his patent he blessed God that he was the first Christian prince that had discovered this land; 2, for that he chargeth him and others with blasphemy for calling Europe Christendom, or the Christian world; 3, for that he did personally apply to our present king, Charles, these three places in the Revelations, viz., [blank].

Mr. Endecott being absent, the governor wrote to him to let him know what was done, and withal added divers arguments to confute the said errors, wishing him to deal with Mr. Williams to retract the same, etc. Whereto he returned a very modest and discreet answer. Mr. Williams also wrote to the governor, and also to him and the rest of the council, very submissively, professing his intent to have been only to have written for the private satisfaction of the governor, etc., of Plymouth, without any purpose to have stirred any further in it, if the governor here had not required a copy of him; withal offering his book, or any part of it, to be burnt.

At the next court he appeared penitently, and gave satisfaction of his intention and loyalty. So it was left, and nothing done in it.

1634

(Nov. 27.) It was likewise informed, that Mr. Williams of Salem had broken his promise to us, in teaching publickly against the king's patent, and our great sin in claiming right thereby to this country, etc., and for usual terming the churches of England antichristian. We granted summons to him for his appearance at the next court.

1635

(April 30.) The governor and assistants sent for Mr. Williams. The occasion was, for that he had taught publicly, that a magistrate ought not to tender an oath to an unregenerate man, for that we thereby have communion with a wicked man in the worship of God, and cause him to take the name of God in vain. He was heard before all the ministers, and very clearly confuted. Mr. Endecott was at first of the same opinion, but he gave place to the truth.

(July 8.) At the general court, Mr. Williams of Salem was summoned, and did appear. It was laid to his charge, that, being under question before the magistracy and churches for divers dangerous opinions, viz. 1, that the magistrate ought not to punish the breach of the first table, otherwise than in such cases as did disturb the civil peace; 2, that he ought not to tender an oath to an unregenerate man; 3, that a man ought not to pray with such, though wife, child, etc.; 4, that a man ought not to give thanks after the sacrament nor after meat, etc.; and that the other churches were about to write to the church of Salem to admonish him of these errors; notwithstanding the church had since called him to [the] office of a teacher. Much debate was about these things. The said opinions were adjudged by all, magistrates and ministers, (who were desired to be present,) to be erroneous, and very dangerous, and the calling of him to office, at that time, was judged a great contempt of authority. So, in fine, time was given to him and the church of Salem to consider of these things till the next general court, and then either to give satisfaction to the court, or else to expect the sentence;, it being professedly declared by the ministers, (at the request of the court to give their advice,) that he who should obstinately maintain such opinions, (whereby a church might run into heresy, apostacy, or tyranny, and yet the civil magistrate could not intermeddle,) were to be removed, and that the other churches ought to request the magistrates so to do.

(July 12.) Salem men had preferred a petition, at the last general court, for some land in Marblehead Neck, which they did challenge as belonging to their town; but, because they had chosen Mr. Williams their teacher, while he stood under question of authority, and so offered contempt to the magistrates, etc., their petition was refused till, etc. Upon this the church of Salem write to other churches, to admonish the magistrates of this as a heinous sin, and likewise the deputies; for which, at the next general court, their deputies were not received until they should give satisfaction about the letter.

(Aug. 16.) Mr. Williams, pastor of Salem, being sick and not able to speak, wrote to his church a protestation, that he could not communicate with the churches in the bay; neither would he communicate with them, except they would refuse communion with the rest; but the whole church was grieved herewith.

(October.) At this general court, Mr. Williams, the teacher at Salem, was again convented, and all the ministers in the bay being desired to be present, he was charged with the said two letters,—that to the churches, complaining of the magistrates for injustice, extreme oppression, etc., and the other to his own church, to persuade them to renounce communion with all the churches in the bay, as full of antichristian pollution, etc. He justified both these letters, and maintained all his opinions; and, being offered further conference or disputation, and a month's respite, he chose to dispute presently. So Mr. Hooker was appointed to dispute with him, but could not reduce him from any of his errors. So, the next morning, the court sentenced him to depart out of our jurisdiction within six weeks, all the ministers, save one, approving the sentence; and his own church had him under question also for the same cause; and he, at his return home, refused communion with his own church, who openly disclaimed his errors, and wrote an humble submission to the magistrates, acknowledging their fault in joining with Mr. Williams in that letter to the churches against them, etc.

1636

(January.) The governor and assistants met at Boston to consider about Mr. Williams, for that they were credibly informed, that, notwithstanding the injunction laid upon him (upon the liberty granted him to stay till the spring) not to go about to draw others to his opinions, he did use to entertain company in his house, and to preach to them, even of such points as he had been censured for; and it was agreed to send him into England by a ship then ready to depart. The reason was, because he had drawn above twenty persons to his opinion, and they were intended to erect a plantation about the Naragansett Bay, from whence the infection would easily spread into these churches, (the people being, many of them, much taken with the apprehension

ιess). Whereupon a warrant im to come presently to Bosipped, etc. He returned answer, (and divers of Salem came with it,) that he could not come without hazard of his life, etc. Whereupon a pinnace was sent with commission to Capt. Underhill, etc., to apprehend him, and carry him aboard the ship, (which then rode at Natascutt;) but, when they came at his house, they found he had been gone three days before; but whither they could not learn.

He had so far prevailed at Salem, as many there (especially of devout women) did embrace his opinions, and separated from the churches, for this cause, that some of their members, going into England, did hear the ministers there, and when they came home the churches here held communion with them.

Roger Williams: Mr. Cotton's Letter Lately Printed, Examined and Answered

Nearly a decade had passed after his banishment when Roger Williams engaged in a remarkable public discussion of all the points which he felt had been at issue between himself and the authorities in Massachusetts. His opponent in this debate was John Cotton, minister of the Boston church. The debate took the form of a series of lengthy letters and books published in England from 1643 to 1652 during the Puritan Revolution in the mother country. The first item to reach the public, much to Cotton's embarrassment, was a letter Cotton had written to Williams shortly after the banishment. Once that letter had been printed, Williams promptly published a reply from which the following selection is taken.

1644

BUT because the Reader may ask both Mr. Cotton and me, what were the grounds of such a sentence of Banishment against me, which are here called sandy, I shall relate in brief what those grounds were, some whereof he is pleased to discuss in this Letter, and others of them not to mention.

After my public trial and answers at the general Court, one of the most eminent Magistrates (whose name and speech may by others be remembered) stood up and spake:

Mr. Williams (said he) holds forth these 4 particulars; First, that we have not our land by patent from the King, but that the natives are the true owners of it, and that we ought to repent of such a receiving it by patent. Secondly, that it is not lawful to call a wicked person to swear, to pray, as being actions of Gods Worship. Thirdly, that it is not lawful to hear any of the ministers of the parish assemblies in England. Fourthly, that the civil magistrates power extends only to the bodies and goods, and outward state of men, etc.

I acknowledge the particulars were rightly summed up, and I also hope, that,

From *Publications of the Narragansett Club* (Providence, 1866), Vol. I, pp. 324–27, 334–35, 392.

as I then maintained the rocky strength of them to my own and other consciences satisfaction so (through the Lords assistance) I shall be ready for the same grounds, not only to be bound and banished, but to die also, in New England, as for most holy truths of God in Christ Jesus.

Yes but (said he) upon those grounds you banished your self from the society of the churches in these countries.

I answer, if Mr. Cotton means my own voluntary withdrawing from those churches resolved to continue in those evils, and persecuting the witnesses of the Lord presenting light unto them, I confess it was my own voluntary act; yea, I hope the act of the Lord Jesus sounding forth in me (a poor despised rams horn) the blast which shall in his own holy season cast down the strength and confidence of those inventions of men in the worshipping of the true and living God. And lastly, his act in enabling me to be faithful in any measure to suffer such great and mighty trials for his names sake. But if by banishing my self he intend the act of civil banishment from their common earth and aire, I then observe with grief the language of the dragon in a lambs lip. Among other expressions of the dragon are not these common to the witnesses of the Lord Jesus rent and torn by his persecutions? Go now, say you are persecuted, you are persecuted for Christ, suffer for your conscience: no, it is your schisme, heresy, obstinacy, the devil hath deceived thee, thou hast justly brought this upon thee, thou hast banished thy self, etc. Instances are abundant in so many books of Martyrs, and the experience of all men, and therefore I spare to recite in so short a treatise.

Secondly, if he mean this civil act of banishing, why should he call a civil sentence from the civil State, within a few weeks execution in so sharp a time of New Englands cold. Why should he call this a banishment from the churches, except he silently confess, that the frame or constitution of their churches is but implicitly national (which yet they profess against) for otherwise why was I not yet permitted to live in the world, or commonwealth, except for this reason, that the commonwealth and church is yet but one, and he that is banished from the one, must necessarily be banished from the other also. . . .

Mr. Cotton. And yet it may be they passed that sentence against you, not upon that ground: but for ought I know, for your other corrupt Doctrines, which tend to the disturbance both of civil and holy peace, as may appear by that answer which was sent to the brethren of the Church of Salem and your self.

I answer, it is no wonder that so many having been demanded the cause of my sufferings have answered, that they could not tell for what, since Mr. Cotton himself knows not distinctly what cause to assign: but said, it may be they passed not that sentence on that ground, etc. Oh, where was the waking care of so excellent and worthy a man, to see his brother and beloved in Christ so afflicted, he knows not distinctly for what.

He alleged a scripture, to prove the sentence righteous, and yet concluded it may be it was not for that, but for other corrupt Doctrines which he named not, nor any Scripture to prove them corrupt, or the sentence righteous for that cause. O that it may please the Father of lights to awaken both himself and other of my honored countrymen, to see how though their hearts wake (in respect of personal grace and life of Jesus) yet they sleep insensible of much concerning the purity of the Lords worship, or the sorrows of such whom they call brethren, and beloved in Christ, afflicted by them.

But though he name not these corrupt doctrines, a little before I have, as they were publicly summed up and charged upon me, and yet none of them tending to the breach of holy or civil peace, of which I have ever desired to be unfainedly tender, acknowledging the Ordinance of Magistracie to be properly and adequately fitted by God, to preserve the civil state in civil peace and order: as he had also appointed a spiritual government and governors in matters pertaining to his worship and the consciences of men, both which governments, governors, laws, offences, punishments, are essentially distinct, and the confounding of them brings all the world into combustion. . . .

Ans. However Mr. Cotton believes and writes of this point, yet has he not duly considered these following particulars:

First the faithful labors of many witnesses of Jesus Christ, extant to the world, abundantly proving, that the Church of the Jews under the Old Testament in the type, and the Church of the Christians under the New Testament in the Antitype, were both separate from the world; and that when they have opened a gap in the hedge or wall of separation between the garden of the church and the wilderness of the world, God hath ever broke down the wall it self, removed the candlestick, etc. and made his garden a wilderness, as at this day. And that therefore if he will ever please to restore his garden and paradise again, it must of necessity be walled in peculiarly unto himself from the world, and that all that shall be saved out of the world are to be transplanted out of the wilderness of world, and added unto his church or garden. . . .

John Cotton: A Reply to Mr. Williams his Examination

Continuing the public debate Cotton, in turn, published a reply to Williams's attack upon his original letter. In the following section Cotton made his most specific defence of the action taken against Williams by the Massachusetts authorities.

1644

THE other part of the chapter, he spent in relating the grounds of the sentence of his banishment, and in the avouchment of his confidence of the firmness of them.

The grounds of the sentence of his banishment, some whereof he says I am pleased to discuss in the Letter, and others not to mention; He said were rightly summed up by one of the magistrates after his public trial, and answers.

Mr. Williams (said that public person) held forth these four particulars.

1. That we have not our land by patent from the King, but that the natives are the true owners of it; and that we ought to repent of such a receiving it by patent.

2. That is is not lawful to call a wicked person to swear, to pray, as being actions of Gods worship.

From *Publications of the Narragansett Club* (Providence, 1867), Vol. 11, pp. 40–57, 183–85.

3. That it is not lawful to hear any of the ministers of the Parish Assemblies in England.

4. That the civil magistrates power extends only to the bodies, and goods, and outward state of men, etc.

These particulars he hoped, that as he maintained the rocky strength of them to his own, and other consciences satisfaction: so (through the Lords assistance,) he shall be ready not only to be bound, and banished, but to die also in New England, as for most holy truths of God in Christ Jesus.

It was not my intent in that letter which he examined, to discuss the grounds of his civil banishment at all, neither did I discuss one or other of them. And it is a preposterous shifting of the state of the question, to put it upon me to give account of the causes of his banishment, who neither did banish him, nor provoked the court to banish him out of the country. The magistrates and deputies of the commonwealth (who were then the members of that court) are all of them of age, and able themselves to give account of their own actions. To them or some of them he should in reason have addressed himself for satisfaction in this case (if any were due) and not to me, who am as seldom present at any civil court, (if not more seldom) than any man of our calling in town or country, where the courts are kept. It were more than Egyptian bondage to me, and more then Pharaonicall tyranny in him, to exact of me, an account of all the capital, or notable sentences of judgement, which pass in all the civil courts of justice in the country, unless I had a calling to sit amongst them.

But why did I then endeavor in my letter to show him the sandiness of those grounds, upon which he had [illegible] himself, etc. if I did not mean to de[illegible] and discuss the causes of his banishme[illegible]

He doth very well, and wisely to express the grounds upon which I said he banished himself with an, etc. For he knows that if he had related my whole sentence in my own words, he had cut off himself from all opportunity of pleading with me the causes of his civil banishment.

My words are plain,—I endeavor to show you the sandiness of those grounds, upon which you have banished your self from the fellowship of all the churches in these countries.

It is one thing to banish ones self (or to be banished) out of the fellowship of all the churches in the country; another thing to banish ones self (or to be banished) out of the country. There be at this day that banish (and separate) themselves from all the churches in the country, and yet are not banished out of the country: and there be that are banished out of the country, and yet are not banished out of the fellowship of all the churches in the country. Himself hath separated (and so banished himself) from the fellowship of all the churches in the world: and yet he hath not banished himself out of the world.

But though it be impertinent to my letter to discuss the grounds of his civil banishment: yet since he is pleased (by hook or crook) to draw it in, I refer the reader for answer to a full treatise of that argument, penned by a reverend faithful brother, (the teacher of the church at Rocksbury;) and withall as I have touched somewhat of it above in answer to his preface, so I shall speak a word or two more unto it here.

Whom that eminent magistrate was, that so summed up the grounds of Mr.

...ent in those four ...ntioned, Mr. Williams ...nceal his name, lest he should be occa...ss against such fraud... of the particulars: ... no causes of his banishment at all, and such as were causes, were not delivered in such general terms. . . . It is evident the two latter causes which he gives of his banishment, were no causes at all, as he expressed them. There are many known to hold both these opinions, that it is not lawful to hear any of the ministers of the parish assemblies in England, and that the civil magistrates power extended only to the bodies, and goods, and outward estates of men: and yet they are tolerated not only to live in the commonwealth, but also in the fellowship of the churches.

The two former, though they be not so much noised, yet there be many, if not most, that hold, that we have not our land, meerly by right of patent from the King, but that the natives are true owners of all that they possess, or improve. Neither do I know any among us, that either then were, or now are of another mind.

And as for the other point; that it is not lawful to call a wicked person to swear, or pray.

Though that be not commonly held, yet it is known to be held of some, who yet are tolerated to enjoy both civil, and church-liberties among us.

To come therefore to particulars: Two things there were, which (to my best observation, and remembrance) caused the sentence of his banishment: and two other fell in, that hastened it.

1. His violent and tumultuous carriage against the patent. By the patent it is, that we received allowance from the King to depart his kingdom, and to carry our goods with us, without offence to his officers, and without paying custom to himself.

By the patent, certain select men (as magistrates, and freemen) have power to make laws, and the magistrates to execute justice, and judgement among the people, according to such laws.

By the patent we have power to erect such a government of the church, as is most agreeable to the word, to the estate of the people, and to the gaining of natives (in Gods time) first to civility, and then to Christianity.

To this authority established by this patent, Englishmen do readily submit themselves: and foreign plantations (the French, the Dutch, and Swedish) do willingly transact their negotiations with us, as with a colony established by the royal authority of the state of England.

This patent, Mr. Williams publicly, and vehemently preached against, as containing matter of falsehood, and injustice: falsehood in making the King the first Christian prince who had discovered these parts: and injustice, in giving the country to his English subjects, which belonged to the native Indians. This therefore he pressed upon the magistrates and people, to be humbled for from time to time in days of solemn humiliation, and to return the patent back again to the King. It was answered to him, first, that it was neither the Kings intendment, nor the English planters to take possession of the country by murder of the natives, or by robbery: but either to take possession of the void places of the country by the law of nature, (for *Vacuum Domicilium cedit occupanti:*) or if we took any lands from the natives, it was by way of purchase, and free consent.

A little before our coming, God had by pestilence, and other contagious diseases, swept away many thousands of the natives, who had inhabited the Bay of Massachusetts, for which the patent was granted. Such few of them as survived were glad of the coming of the English, who might preserve them from the oppression of the Nahargansets. For it is the manner of the natives, the stronger nations to oppress the weaker.

This answer did not satisfy Mr. Williams, who pleaded, the natives, though they did not, nor could subdue the country, (but left it *vacuum Domicilium*) yet they hunted all the country over, and for the expedition of their hunting voyages, they burnt up all the underwoods in the country, once or twice a year, and therefore as noble men in England possessed great parkes, and the King, great forests in England only for their game, and no man might lawfully invade their propriety: So might the natives challenge the like propriety of the country here.

It was replied unto him. 1. That the King, and noble men in England, as they possessed greater territories than other men, so they did greater service to church, and commonwealth. 2. That they employed their parks, and forests, not for hunting only, but for timber, and for the nourishment of tame beasts, as well as wild, and also for habitation to sundry tenants. 3. That our towns here did not disturb the huntings of the natives, but did rather keep their game fitter for their taking; for they take their deer by traps, and not by hounds. 4. That if they complained of any straites we put upon them, we gave satisfaction in some payments, or other, to their content. 5. We did not conceive that it is a just title to so vast a continent, to make no other improvement of millions of acres in it, but only to burn it up for pastime.

But these answers not satisfying him, this was still pressed by him as a national sin, to hold to the patent, yea, and a national duty to renounce the patent: which to have done, had subverted the fundamental state, and government of the country.

2. The second offence, which procured his banishment, was occasioned as I touched before. The magistrates, and other members of the general court upon intelligence of some Episcopal, and malignant practises against the country, they made an order of court to take trial of the fidelity of the people, (not by imposing upon them, but) by offering to them an oath of fidelity: that in case any should refuse to take it, they might not betrust them with place of public charge, and command. This oath when it came abroad, he vehemently withstood it, and dissuaded sundry from it, partly because it was, as he said, Christ's prerogative, to have his office established by oath: partly because an oath was a part of God's worship, and God's worship was not to be put upon carnal persons, as he conceived many of the people to be. So by his tenent neither might church-members, nor other godly men, take the oath, because it was the establishment not of Christ, but of mortal men in their office; nor might men out of the church take it, because in his eye they were but carnal. So the court was forced to desist from that proceeding: which practise of his was held to be the more dangerous, because it tended to unsettle all the kingdoms, and commonwealths in Europe.

These were (as I took it) the causes of his banishment: two other things fell in upon these that hastened the sentence. The former fell out thus: the magistrates discerning by the former passages, the heady and turbulent spirit of Mr. Williams, both they, and others advised the Church of Salem not to call him to office in their church; nevertheless, the major part of the church made choice of him. Soon after, when the church made suit to the court for a parcel of land adjoining to them, the court delayed to grant their request (as hath been mentioned before) because the church had refused to hearken to the magistrates, and others in forbearing the choice of Mr. Williams. Whereupon Mr. Williams took occasion to stir up the church to join with him in writing Letters of Admonition unto all the churches, whereof those magistrates were members, to admonish them of their open transgression of the rule of justice. Which letters coming to the several churches, provoked the magistrates to take the more speedy course with so heady, and violent a spirit.

But to prevent his sufferings, (if it might be) it was moved by some of the elders, that themselves might have liberty (according to the Rule of Christ) to deal with him, and with the church also in a church-way. It might be, the church might hear us, and he the church; which being consented to, some of our churches wrote to the church of Salem, to present before them the offensive spirit, and way of their officer, (Mr. Williams) both in judgement, and practise. The church finally began to hearken to us, and accordingly began to address themselves to the healing of his spirit. Which he discerning, renounced communion with the church of Salem, pretending they held communion with the churches in the bay, and the churches in the bay held communion with the parish-churches in England, because they suffered their members to hear the word amongst them in England, as they came over into their native country. He then refusing to resort to the public assembly of the church. Soon after sundry began to resort to his family, where he preached to them on the Lords day. But this carriage of his in renouncing the church upon such an occasion, and with them all the churches in the country, and the spreading of his leaven to sundry that resorted to him; this gave the magistrates the more cause to observe the heady unruliness of his spirit, and the incorrigibleness thereof by any church-way, all the churches in the country being then renounced by him. And this was the other occasion which hastened the sentence of his banishment, upon the former grounds.

If upon these grounds Mr. Williams be ready, (as he professeth) not only to be bound, and banished, but also to die in New England; let him remember, (what he knows) *Non poena, sed causa facit Martyrem;* No Martyr of Christ did ever suffer for such a cause. . . .

But thus have I opened the grounds, and occasions of his civil banishment; which whether they be sandy, or rocky, let the servants of Christ judge. Howsoever, my letter gave him no occasion at all to put me upon this discourse; for in my letter I intended only to show him the sandiness of those grounds upon which he banished himself from the society (not of the commonwealth, but) of all the churches in these countries.

But whether I intended the one, or the other, he giveth an answer for both; If Mr. Cotton mean (saith he) my own voluntary withdrawing from all these churches resolved to continue in those evils, and in persecuting the witnesses of the Lord, presenting light unto them, I confess it was mine own voluntary act: yea I hope the act of the Lord Jesus sounding forth in me (a poor despised Rams-horn) the blast which shall in his own holy season cast down the strength, and confidence of the inventions of men in the worship of God: and lastly his act in inabling me to be faithful in any measure to suffer such great, and mighty trials for his Names sake.

Reply, that I meant only his own act in withdrawing himself from these churches, doth plainly enough appear both from my express words, and from the reasons which I expressly assign of that act of his, which I called the sandy grounds, upon which he builds his separation. My express words are, He had banished himself from the society of all the churches in this country. The society of the church is one thing, the society of the commonwealth, is another. And the grounds upon which he built his separation, were not the causes of his banishment, but of his withdrawing from the society of the churches.

But if I so meant, he confesseth it was his own voluntary act; and professeth also, it was a double act of the Lord Jesus in him.

The ground which he giveth of his own voluntary act, was because these churches were resolved to continue in those evils, and persecuting the witnesses of the Lord Jesus, presenting light to them.

Reply; Those evils? What were those evils, which we were resolved to continue in? He expresseth none: but sure meet it had been, that as his voluntary withdrawing from these churches was publicly known; so the evils in which we resolved to continue, and for which he withdrew himself, should in like manner have been publicly known also. It is an unrighteous thing to pass public known acts, upon private unknown evils. But whatsoever those unknown evils were, I suppose he conceiveth them to be such ways, either of judgement, or practise, wherein we walk according to the light of our consciences. And then by his rule he should have allowed us the like liberty of conscience, which himself requireth. And surely by the Royal Rule of the Lord Jesus, no brother may be so much as admonished, (much less separated from) till he be convinced, Mat. 18. 15.

And as for persecuting the witnesses of the Lord, presenting light to us; himself (for ought I know) was the first in this country that ever pretended suffering for bearing witness in any matter of religion true or false: And for him to withdraw himself from the society of all the churches for their persecution of him, before he had suffered from them any thing but conference, and conviction, is to make them sufferers for well-doing, and to chose suffering, that he might have cause to complain of sufferings. Let him, if he be able, name any one in this country of the witnesses of the Lord, (for he speaketh of witnesses) that ever did so much as pretend before himself to suffer persecution, for presenting light to us. . . .

Again, he recoileth to his civil banishment, and observeth, That if by banishing himself I meant his civil banishment, then 1. He discerneth the language of the dragon in a lambs lip; to put the sufferings of the Saints upon themselves, and the devil. 2. That I silently confess, that the frame and constitution of our churches is implicitly national. Else if the commonwealth, and church were not one, how could he that is banished from the one, be necessarily banished from the other also?

Reply. It was far from my meaning, and words, when I spake of his banishing of himself from the fellowship of all the churches in the country, to intend his civil banishment. I knew his civil banishment was not merely his own act. I knew also that he might have been banished from the commonwealth, and yet have retained (as some others have done) fellowship with some churches, if not with all the churches in the country. And therefore both his observations are but empty flourishes, and vanish like bubbles. It is the wiliness of the spirit of the serpent, to hide his head under fig-leaved evasions.

But suppose I had meant by his banishment of himself, his civil banishment, and had meant, that by exposing himself deservedly to that censure, he had deprived himself of enjoying all the spiritual liberties of the churches in the country: might I not so have said, and yet not have spoken the language of the dragon? What if the dragon use such language to the Saints suffering innocently? may not the spirit of God use the same words to a guilty person suffering deservedly? The language of the dragon lyeth not always in the words or meaning, but in the application, and intent of them. The dragon said to Christ, I know who thou art, the holy one of God, Mar. 1. 24. Peter might say the same, or the like words, Mat. 16. 16. And yet in his mouth, it was not the language of the dragon, but of the Holy Ghost.

Neither will it imply, that the church, and commonwealth, are all one, because he that deservedly is banished from the commonwealth, banisheth himself also from the communion of the churches; for the same sins which may be offensive civilly to the commonwealth, may be also spiritually offensive to the church, and both proceed to censure the same person in their own way, severally. . . .

But, saith he, if it be butchery to separate conscientiously and peaceably from the spiritual communion of a church, or Saints, what shall it be called by the Lord Jesus, to cut off persons, them, and theirs, branch, and root, from any civil being in their territories, etc. Because their consciences dare not bow down to any worship, but what the Lord Jesus hath appointed, and being also otherwise subject to the civil estate, and laws thereof?

Here be many extenuations, and mincings of his own carriage, and as many false aggravations of guilt upon his sentence of banishment, and the authors of it.

As, 1. In that he was cut off, he and his, branch and root, from any civil being in these territories, because their consciences durst not bow down to any worship, but what they believe the Lord had appointed: Whereas the truth is, his banishment proceeded not against him, or his, for his own refusal of any worship, but for seditious opposition against the patent, and against the oath of fidelity offered to the people.

2. That he was subject to the civil estate, and laws thereof, when yet he vehemently opposed the civil foundation of the civil estate, which was the patent: and earnestly also opposed the law of the general court, by which the tender of that oath was enjoined: and also wrote letters of admonition to all the churches, whereof the magistrates were members, for deferring to give present answer to a petition of Salem, who had refused to hearken to a lawful motion of theirs.

3. That he did but separate from the spiritual society of a church, or Saints: whereas he both drew away many others also, and as much as in him lay, separated all the churches from Christ.

4. In that he maketh the cutting off of

persons, them and theirs, branch and rush, from civil territories, a far more heinous and odious offence in the eyes of the Lord Jesus, than himself to cut off, not only himself and his, branch and rush, but many of his neighbors (by sedition) from spiritual communion with the churches, and all the churches from communion with Christ. As if the cutting of persons, them and theirs, branch and rush, from the covenant, and spiritual ordinances in the church, were a matter of no account in respect of cutting off from civil liberties in the territories of the commonwealth.

5. In that, what himself did, he predicated as done conscientiously and peaceably, as if what the court had done against him, they had not done conscientiously also, and with regard to public peace, which they saw he disturbed, and stood stiffly in his own course, though he was openly convinced in open court (as I showed before) that he could not maintain his way, but by sinning against the light of his own conscience.

Roger Williams: The Bloody Tenent Yet More Bloody

In addition to the three published letters by Cotton and Williams, the two opponents printed three books containing more extended and general arguments over the question of liberty of conscience and the proper nature of the church. These were the famous "bloody" books: 1.) The Bloudy Tenent *by Williams; 2.)* The Bloudy Tenent, Washed, And made white in the bloud of the Lambe *by Cotton; and 3.)* The Bloody Tenent yet More Bloody *by Williams. This final volume included an opening plea by Williams "To the Several Respective General Courts, especially that of the Massachusetts in New England," a plea which is excerpted here.*

1647

WHILE you sit dry on your safe American shoars (by God's most gracious Providence) and have beheld the dolefull tossings of so many of Europe's nations, yea of our dearest Mother, aged England, in a sea of tears and blood, I am humbly bold to present your eyes and hearts with this (not unseasonable) discourse of blood, of the bloody tenents of persecution, oppression, and violence, in the cause and matters of conscience and religion.

It is a second conference of peace and truth, an examination of the worthily honored and beloved Mr. Cotton's reply to a former conference and treatise of this subject. And although it concern all nations, which have persecuted and shed the blood of Jesus, the bloody Roman Empire, with all the savage lions thereof, emperors and popes, the bloody monarchies of Spain and France, and the rest of Europe's kingdoms and states (which under their several vizards and pretences's of service to God, have in so many thousands of his servants, murdered so many thousand times over, his dear son) yea although it concern that bloody Turkish monarchy, and all the na-

From *Publications of the Narragansett Club* (Providence, 1870), Vol. IV, pp. 23–32.

tions of the world who practise violence to the conscience of any Christian, or Anti-christians, Jews or Pagans; yet it concerns your selves (with all due respect otherwise be it spoken) in some more eminent degrees: partly as so many of yours of chief note (beside Mr. Cotton) are engaged in it; partly as New England (in respect of spiritual and civil state) professeth to draw nearer to Christ Jesus then other states and churches, and partly as New England is believed to hold and practise such a bloody doctrine, notwithstanding Mr. Cotton's vails and pretences of not persecuting men for conscience, but punishing them only for sinning against conscience and of but so and so, not persecuting, but punishing heretics, blasphemers, idolators, seducers, etc. . . .

Without remembering therefore who my adversary is, nor all the wormwood and the gall so frequently in Mr. Cotton's reply against me; I fully and only level with an upright and single eye (the Lord Jesus graciously assisting) against that fowl and monstrous bloody tenent and doctrine, which hath so slyly (like the old serpent the author of it) crept under the shade and shelter of Mr. Cotton's patronage and protection.

My end is to discover and proclaim the crying and horrible guilt of the bloody doctrine, as one of the most seditious, destructive, blasphemous, and bloodiest in any or in all the nations of the world, notwithstanding the many fine vails, pretences and colors of not persecuting Christ Jesus, but heretics, not God's truth or servants, but blasphemers, seducers: not persecuting men for their conscience, but for sinning against their conscience, etc. . . .

My end and scope is to put a Christian bar, and just and merciful spokes in the wheels of such zealous reforming Jews, who (under the vizard and name of Baals Priests) may possibly be induced to account it good service unto God, to kill and burn his precious servants. . . .

My truly honoured and beloved countrymen, vouchsafe me I beseech you that humane and Christian liberty to say, that I fear your spirits are locked up in a double prison from any serious audience to ought of mine presented to you. The first of prejudice against such and such a person. The second of conscience, against such and such a matter; and that while my conscience or another man's faith, let me be heretic, blasphemer, idolater, seducer, with Christ Jesus, with his Apostles, Saints and Witnesses: Let me (for his sake) bear frowns, censures, and persecutions, from men so dear, so excellent, so holy! Your consciences plead for equal liberty of opposing in your way, all such erroneous or wandering consciences.

For answer, it is but humanity, it is but Christianity to exercise meekness and moderation to all men: It is humane and Christian wisdom to listen to a serious alarm against a common enemy: Prove the alarm false, it may be but troublesome: Prove it true, it may be destruction to have despised it.

As the wounds of a lover are better then the kisses of an enemy: so saith the same spirit, an open rebuke is better then secret love. [Proverbs, xxvii: 5.]

But yet your consciences (as all mens) must be satisfied, I have therefore in all these agitations humbly presented (amongst others) two fundamental hints or considerations:

First that the people (the original of all free power and government) are not invested with power from Christ Jesus, to rule his wife or church, to keep it pure, to punish opposites by force of armes, etc.

Secondly, that the pattern of the national church of Israel, was a none-such, unimitable by any civil state, in all or any of the nations of the world beside. . . .

I add, it is a glorious character of every true disciple or scholar of Christ Jesus, to be never too old to learn.

It is the command of Christ Jesus to his scholars, to try all things: and liberty of trying what a friend, yea what an (esteemed) enemie presents, hath ever (in point of Christianity) proved one especial means of attaining to the truth of Christ.

For I dare confidently appeal to the consciences of God's most knowing servants, if that observation be not true, to wit, that it hath been the common way of the Father of Lights, to inclose the light of his holy truths, in dark and obscure, yea and ordinarily in forbidden books, persons and meetings, by Satan stiled conventicles.

New English Voyages, have taught most of our old English spirits, how to put due prices upon the most common and ordinary undervalued mercies; how precious with some hath been a little water? how dainty with others a piece of bread: How welcome to some the poorest housing? Yea the very land and earth, after long and tedious passages?

There is one commodity for the sake of which most of God's children in New England have run their mighty hazards; a commodity marvelously scarce in former times (though in some late years by God's most gracious and mighty hand more plentiful) in our native country: It is a liberty of searching after God's most holy mind and pleasure.

Out of this most precious and invaluable jewel, if you suffer Satan (that grand thief and cheater) to bereave you, and that it shall be a crime, humbly and peaceably to question even laws and statutes, or what ever is even publicly taught and delivered, you will most certainly find your selves after all your long run (like that little Frenchman who killed the Duke of Guise, and was taken next morning near the place from whence he had fled upon a swift horse all night) I say you will most certainly find your selves, but where you were, enslaved and captivated in the chains of those popish darknesses, [to wit, Ignorance is the mother of Devotion, and we must believe as the church believes, etc.]

Remember therefore (O ye the cream and flower of English plantations in America) what a black and direfull a cole it was with which it pleased the spirit of God in Habacuck, to brand the Assirian monarchie to wit [a bitter and hastie nation] but in the spirit of meekness, in the meekness of wisdom, be pleased to remember that possible it is for Gods visible, only people in the world to have very foul and bloody hands, full of blood (Isa. I.)! To build up Zion and Jerusalem (that is, to erect the visible church and Kingdom of God) with blood (Mic. 3.) and with iniquity: That the heads and judges of God's people, may judge for a reward (and the deceitful heart of man graspeth at rewards more then of one sort) that the priests and prophets thereof may teach and prophesie (and it may be frequently and excellently, but yet for) an hire and for money; and that yet their consciences may lean upon Jehovah, and they may say with confidence, is not the Lord amongst us? None evil shall come unto us; etc. O remember that your gifts are rare, your professions of religion (in such way) rare, your persecutions and hidings from the storms abroad, rare and wonderful: So in proportion your transgressions, estate and public sins cannot but be of a rare and extraordinary guilt: Nor will New England's sorrowes (when sins are ripe and full) be other then the dregs of Germany's, of Ireland's, of England's, and of Scotland's Tears and Calamities.

Amongst the crying sins of our own or other sinful nations: those two are ever amongst the loudest, to wit, invented devotions to the God of Heaven. Secondly, violence and oppression on the sons of men (especially if his sons) for dissenting, and against both these, and that the impartial and dreadfull hand of the most holy and Jealous God (a consuming fire) tear and burn not up at last the roots of these plantations, but graciously discovering the plants which are not his, he may graciously fructifie and cause to flourish what his right hand will own: I say this is the humble and unfeigned desire and cry (at the throne of grace) of your so long despised Out-cast.

PART II. HOW THE CASE OF ROGER WILLIAMS APPEARED TO A MASSACHUSETTS HISTORIAN IN 1702

Cotton Mather: MAGNALIA CHRISTI AMERICANA

The most vigorous and vehement condemnation of Roger Williams appears in Cotton Mather's extensive history of the New England churches. A grandson of John Cotton, Mather wrote his history in 1702 to recall third-generation Puritans to "the faith of their fathers"—but ran the risk of calling them to worship their fathers more than their fathers' God. Perry Miller describes this passage as "vibrant with suppressed meanings."

1702

LITTLE FOXES: or, the Spirit of Rigid Separation in one Remarkable Zealot, vexing the Churches of New England.

Hic se aperit Diabolus!

1. It is remarkable, that in the sacred annals of that matchless and blessed church-history, which our God has given us in our Bible, there is a special mark often set upon the first persons that were eminent in this or that way of sinning, and were upon that score, *the chief of sinners;* and they who have observed this remarkable, have particularly marked the infamous Corah, the *first rebel* against the divine church-order established in the wilderness, as one instance to confirm the observation. There are some, not thoughtless persons, who innumerating the troublesome and scandalous things that have disturbed us in our New-English wilderness, have complained of a crime, which they have distinguished by the name of CORAHISM; or that litigious and levelling spirit, with which the *separation* has been leavened. Now tho' I would chuse rather to leave a veil than a scar upon the memory of any person, that by his miscarriage hath made himself too memorable; yet our church-history will be but an unfinished piece, if we do not set a mark upon that man who was one of the first that made themselves notable by their opposition to the church-order of these plantations; and this we may the more freely do, because of an injunction upon us, *to mark them that cause divisions.*

2. In the year 1654, a certain Windmill in the Low Countries, whirling round with extraordinary violence, by reason of a violent storm then blowing; the stone at length by its rapid motion became so intensely hot, as to fire the mill, from whence the flames, being dispersed by the high winds, did set a whole town on fire. But I can tell my reader, that about twenty years before this, there was

From *Magnalia Christi Americàna or, The Ecclesiastical History of New England,* Book VII, Chap. 2, "The Little Foxes."

a whole country in America like to be set on fire by the rapid motion of a windmill, in the head of one particular man. Know then, that about the year 1630, arrived here one Mr. *Roger Williams;* who being a preacher that had less light than fire in him, hath by his own sad example, preached unto us the danger of that evil which the apostle mentions in Rom. 10. 2. *They have a zeal, but not according to knowledge.* Upon his arrival, the church of Salem, invited him to assist Mr. Skelton in the charge of their souls; but the governour and council fearing lest not only that church would soon come to have nothing of Salem in it, but also that the whole political, as well as ecclesiastical constitution of the country, would suffer by employing a minister of his character, did advise them to desist from laying hands too suddenly upon him. And that which increased in them the suspicion of his ill character, was partly, indeed, his refusing to communicate with the church of Boston, because they would not make a publick and solemn declaration of repentance, for their communicating with the church of England, while they were in the realm of England; (which the New-English reformers thought then would be to carry the matter as far beyond their sense, as the vulgar translation hath done to the text in Luke 15. 8. where, instead of *everrit domum,* she *swept* the house; it reads, *evertit domum,* or, she *overset* it:) but partly his violent urging, that the civil magistrate might not punish breaches of the first table in the laws of the ten commandments; which assertion, besides the door which it opened unto a thousand profanities, by not being duly limited, it utterly took away from the authority all capacity to prevent the land, which they had purchased on purpose for their own recess from such things, its becoming such a sink of abominations, as would have been the reproach and ruin of christianity in these parts of the world. The church taking the advice of their fathers in the State, on this occasion Mr. Williams removed unto Plymouth, where he was accepted as a preacher for the two years ensuing.

3. But at Plymouth his turbulent and singular opinions, not finding the entertainment which he expected, he desired a dismission back to Salem from them; and they perceiving the giddy courses of *separation,* whereto he would abandon himself, and whereby he might endanger them, wisely humour'd what he desir'd. Coming to Salem, in the time of Mr. Skelton's illness, the church, affected with the fierceness of his talking in publick, and the starchtness of his living in private, so far forgot themselves, as to renew their invitations unto him to become their pastor; and tho' the government again renewed their advice unto the people to forbear a thing of such ill consequence, yet they rashly pursued their motion, and he quickly accepted it. It happened that soon after this, the church made suit unto the court for a parcel of land, which lay commodious for their affairs; but the court offended at the slight lately put upon them, delay'd their grant of what the church petitioned for; whereupon, incensed Mr. Williams enchants the church to join with him, in writing letters of admonition unto all the churches, whereof any of the magistrates were members, that they might admonish the magistrates of scandalous injustice for denying this petition. The neighbouring churches, both by petitions and messengers, took such happy pains with the church of Salem, as presently recovered that holy flock to a sense of his aberrations; which Mr. Williams perceiving, tho' he had a little before bragg'd, *that of*

all the churches in the world, those of New-England were the purest; and of all in New-England, that whereof himself was the teacher; yet he now staying at home, sent unto the church of Salem, then assembled, a letter, to give them notice, *that if they would not separate as well from the churches of New-England, as of old, he would separate from them.* His more considerate church not yielding to these lewd proposals, he never would come to their assemblies any more; no, nor hold any *communion* in any exercise of religion with any person, so much as his own wife, that went up unto their assemblies; but at the same time he kept a meeting in his own house, whereto resorted such as he had infected with his extravagancies.

4. These things were, indeed, very disturbant and offensive; but there were two other things in his quixotism, that made it no longer convenient for the civil authority to remain unconcerned about him. For, first, whereas the king of England had granted a royal charter unto the governour and company of this colony; which patent was indeed the very life, of the colony; this hot-headed man publickly and furiously preached against the patent, as an instrument of injustice, and pressed both rulers and people to be humbled for their sin in taking such a patent, and utterly throw it up; on an insignificant pretence of wrong thereby done unto the Indians, which were the natives of the country, therein given to the subjects of the English crown. Secondly, an order of the court, upon some just occasion had been made, that an oath of fidelity should be though not imposed upon, yet offered unto the freemen, the better to distinguish those whose fidelity might render them capable of imployment in the government: which order this man vehemently withstood, on a pernicious pretence, that it was the prerogative of our Lord Christ alone to have his office established with an oath; and that an oath being the worship of God, carnal persons, whereof he supposed there were many, in the land, might not be put upon it. These crimes at last procured a sentence of banishment upon him.

5. The court, about a year before they proceeded unto the banishment of this incendiary, sent for the pastors of the neighbouring churches, to intimate unto them their design of, thus proceeding against him; which yet they were loth to do, before they had advised the elders of it, because he was himself an elder. Mr. Cotton, with the consent of the other ministers, presented a request unto the magistrates, that they would please to forbear prosecuting of him, till they themselves, with their churches, had in a church-way endeavoured his conviction and repentance; for they alledged, that they hoped his violences proceeded rather from a misguided-conscience, than from a seditious principle. The governour foretold unto them, *you are deceived in the man, if you think he will condescend to learn of any of you;* however the proposal of the ministers was approved and allowed. But several of the churches having taken the best pains they could, tho' they happily brought the church of Salem to join with them in dealing with the man, yet the effect was, that he renounced them all, as *no churches* of our Lord Jesus Christ. Whereupon the court ordered his removal out of the jurisdiction.

6. One passage that happened at his trial was a little odd. He complained in open court that he was wronged by a slanderous report, as if he *held it unlawful for a father to call upon his child to eat his meat.*

Mr. Hooker then present, being moved hereupon to speak something, replied, *Why? You will say as much again, if you stand to your own principles, or be driven to say nothing at all.* Mr. Williams expressing his confidence that he should never say it; Mr. Hooker proceeded; *If it be unlawful to call an unregenerate person to pray, since it is an action of God's worship, then it is unlawful for your unregenerate child to pray for a blessing upon his own meat. If it be unlawful for him to pray for a blessing upon his meat, it is unlawful for him to eat it, for it is sanctified by prayer, and without prayer, unsanctified:* [1 Tim. 4.4,5.] *If it be unlawful for him to eat it, it is unlawful for you to call upon him to eat it; for it is unlawful for you to call upon him to sin.* Hereupon Mr. Williams chose to hold his peace, rather than make any answer: such the giddiness, the confusion, the antocatacritic of that sectarian spirit. I have read of a gentleman who had an humour of making singular and fanciful expositions of scripture, but one Doctor Sim gave him a dose of physick, which when it had wrought, the gentleman became orthodox immediately, and expounded at the old rate no more. Pity this Dr. Sim had but undertaken the cure of our Mr. Williams.

7. Upon the sentence of the court, Mr. Williams with his party going abroad (as one says) to *seek their providences*, removed into the Southern parts of New-England, where he, with a few of his own sect settled a place called Providence. There they proceeded not only unto the gathering of a thing like a church, but unto the renouncing of their infant-baptism; and at this further step of *separation* they stopped not, but Mr. Williams quickly told them, *that being himself misled, he had led them likewise out of the way;* he was now satisfied, that there was none upon earth that could administer baptism, and so that their last baptism, as well as their first was a nullity, for the want of a called administration; he advised them therefore to forego all, to dislike every thing, and wait for the coming of new apostles; whereupon they dissolved themselves, and became that sort of sect which we term Seekers, keeping to that one principle, *that every one should have the liberty to worship God according to the light of his own conscience;* but owning of no true churches or ordinances now in the world. It is a memorable reflection made on this occasion by Mr. Cotton, in a book which he published for his own vindication from the printed calumnies of Mr. Williams: "It is a wise proverb," saith he, "of a wiser than Solomon; the backslider in heart (from any truth or way of God) shall be filled with his own ways. They that separate from their brethren further than they have just cause, shall at length find cause, or at least think they have found cause just enough to separate from one another. I never yet heard of any instance to the contrary, either in England or Holland; and for New-England, there is no such church of the separation at all that I know of. That separate church, (if it may be called a church) which separated with Mr. Williams, first broke into a division about a small occasion (as I have heard) and then broke forth into Anabaptism, and then into Antibaptism and Familism, and now finally into no church at all."

8. Mr. Williams after this was very instrumental in obtaining a charter for the government of Rhode-Island, which lay near and with his town of Providence, and was by the people sometimes chosen governour: but for the most part he led a more private life.

It was more than forty years after his

exile that he lived here, and in many things acquitted himself so laudably, that many judicious persons judged him to have had the *root of the matter* in him, during the long winter of this retirement: He used many commendable endeavours to Christianize the Indians in his neighbourhood, of whose language, tempers and manners he printed a little relation with observations, wherein he spiritualizes the curiosities with two and thirty chapters, whereof he entertains his reader. There was always a good correspondence always held between him and many worthy and pious people in the colony, from whence he had been vanish'd tho' his keeping still so many of his dangerous principles, kept the government, unto whose favour some of the English nobility had by letters recommended him, from taking off the sentence of his banishment. And against the Quakers, he afterwards maintained the main principles of the protestant religion with much vigour in some disputations; whereof he afterwards published a large account, in a book against George Fox and Edward Burrowes, which he entituled, *George Fox digg'd out of his burrowes.* But having reported thus much concerning Mr. Williams, we shall now supersede further mention of him, with the mention of another difference which happened in our primitive times, wherein he was (indeed but obliquely and remotely) concerned.

PART III. OPPOSING NINETEENTH-CENTURY VIEWS ON THE MEANING OF THE BANISHMENT OF ROGER WILLIAMS

James D. Knowles: MEMOIR OF ROGER WILLIAMS

The Baptists looked upon Roger Williams as an early hero of their denomination, and it was a Baptist minister, the Rev. James D. Knowles, who wrote the first extended biography of Williams in 1834. Striving to be fair-minded to the Puritans, Knowles nevertheless saw the controversy as a very simple one over the principle of liberty of conscience.

WHAT was there, then, it may be inquired, in the opinions of Mr. Williams, which was so offensive to the rulers in church and state? His denial of the right to possess the lands of the Indians without their own consent, needed not to disturb the colonists, for they purchased their lands from the natives. His ideas of the unlawfulness of oaths, and of the impropriety of praying with unregenerate persons, and other harmless notions of this kind, were surely too unimportant to excite the fears and provoke the ire of the government. We are led to the conclusion, that the cause of Mr. Williams' banishment is to be found in the great principle which has immortalized his name, that THE CIVIL POWER HAS NO JURISDICTION OVER THE CONSCIENCE. This noble doctrine, which the Scriptures clearly teach, and which reason itself proclaims, was, at that time, viewed, by most men, to be as heterodox, in morals, as the Copernican theory was considered by the Inquisition to be false in philosophy; and he who maintained it was liable to the fate of Galileo. The Papists abhorred it, for it would have subverted the Papal throne. The English Church rejected it, for it would have wrested from the hierarchy its usurped authority, and led the Church away from the throne of an earthly monarch to the footstool of the King of kings, as her only head and sovereign. The Puritans themselves disowned it, for they were so firmly convinced of the truth of their doctrines, that they deemed him, who was so obstinate as not to embrace them, to be worthy of punishment for acting in opposition to his own conscience. They refused to conform to the ceremonies of the English Church, but it was because they believed those ceremonies to be idolatrous, and not because they denied to men the power to enforce the belief of doctrines and the practice of rites. They opposed the Prelates, but they believed that a similar sway might be safely intrusted to their own hands. They resisted and for a while triumphed over the Lords Bishops, but they forgot that the despotism of the Lords Brethren, as Blackstone termed them, might be quite as intolerable. They did not understand the nature of that liberty which the Gospel bestows. They were misled by the analogies which they drew from the Mosaic institutions, and felt it to be their duty to extirpate heresy, with as unsparing rigor, as the Jews were required to exercise against those who despised or violated their ritual.

The character of the Puritans has been greatly misunderstood on this point, and there has been much commonplace declamation respecting their bigotry and inconsistency in persecuting others, after having suffered persecution themselves. But a candid mind, which understands their principles, will not, while it must lament and condemn their conduct, use the language of harsh censure. They were so far from believing, that liberty of conscience in religious concerns ought to be extended to all men, that they regarded toleration as a crime. They argued, that they ought to promote truth, and oppose error, by all the methods in their power. If they were able to suppress false doctrines, it was, they believed, a solemn duty to God to employ force, if necessary, for their suppression. They thought, that he who permitted error to be believed and preached, was chargeable with a participation in the guilt. Intolerance became, in their view, a paramount duty to God and to the heretic himself; and the greater their love of God and of truth, the greater was their zeal to extirpate, with a strong hand, every noxious weed from the garden of the Lord. It was not, therefore, a bigoted preference merely for their own views which made them persecute others, but a conviction that they only embraced the truth, and that all opposing doctrines were pernicious, and must not be allowed. It was not, in their judgment, inconsistent to act thus towards others, after having themselves endured persecution; for they regarded themselves as having been sufferers for the truth, and they were urged, by these very sufferings, to be more faithful in upholding that truth, and suppressing what they deemed to be error. It is due to the Pilgrims to remember, that they acted from principles, erroneous certainly, and deplorable in their effects, but sincerely adopted and cherished in hearts which, nevertheless, glowed with love to God. The grand doctrine of LIBERTY OF CONSCIENCE was then a portentous novelty, and it was the glory of Roger Williams, that he, in such an age, proclaimed it, defended it, suffered for it, and triumphantly established it.

The principles of Roger Williams stood in the attitude of irreconcilable opposition to the system which the Pilgrims had established in New-England. They could not blend with it. They came into collision with it, at every point. We have accordingly seen, that Mr. Williams was continually at variance with the government, because their measures were adjusted to their settled policy, but were repugnant to his great doctrine. There could be no peace between them, unless he yielded, or they abandoned their system. He was firm, and they were unconvinced. They possessed the power, and they banished him; not so much to punish him, as to remove from the colony a man whose doctrines they believed to be wrong, whose influence they feared, and whom they could neither intimidate nor persuade to abandon his principles.

It is intimated by Dr. Bentley, that the rivalry of Salem and Boston had some effect to induce a rigorous treatment of Mr. Williams. He had great influence in Salem. He had drawn thither some persons from Plymouth, and it was, perhaps, feared, that his popularity gave an importance to Salem, which might be prejudicial to the metropolis.

It is due to the principal actors in

s, to record the fact, of which dence exists, that personal ani- ad little, if any, share in produc- ing sentence of banishment. Towards Mr. Williams, as a Christian and a minister, there was a general sentiment of respect. Governor Winthrop was a generous friend to him throughout his life; and it is asserted by Dr. Bentley, that "had Governor Winthrop been at liberty to concur with Endicott, and not have been deterred by the competition of Boston and Salem, Williams would have lived and died at Salem."

Mr. Haynes was Governor at the time Mr. Williams was banished, and Mr. Winthrop lost for a while his salutary influence over the public councils. He endeavored, at a subsequent period, to procure a repeal of the sentence of banishment against Mr. Williams; but a more rigid policy prevailed, and the founder of Rhode-Island continued till his death an outlaw from Massachusetts.

Mr. Cotton was, at that time, the most powerful man in the commonwealth; and well did his piety, learning and intrepid love of pure religion merit the respect and affections of the colonists. Whatever share he may have had in procuring the banishment of Mr. Williams, it is certain, that there was no personal feud between them. They had been acquainted with each other in England, and had alike suffered from the intolerance of the Prelates. Mr. Cotton sincerely thought Mr. Williams' principles wrong, and dangerous to the church and the state. He felt it to be the duty of the government to protect the colony, by removing from it this source of peril. In the controversy which subsequently arose between Mr. Cotton and Mr. Williams, the latter uniformly spoke of Mr. Cotton in the most respectful terms; a circumstance, which is the more remarkable, because at that day the style of polemic discussion was less decorous than it is at the present time, and disputants lavished upon each other, with unsparing virulence, the bitterest epithets of obloquy. While we lament, therefore, that a man of so many admirable qualities as Mr. Cotton, was misled by wrong views of religious liberty, and thus betrayed into intolerance, we owe it to his honorable fame to remember, that the best men are imperfect, and that no personal hostility inflamed his zeal.

We may express the verdict, which, at this distant period, all calm and fair minds will, it is presumed, pronounce: that Mr. Williams was unnecessarily scrupulous about some minor points of conduct and of policy, though these scruples may be candidly traced to the agitated condition of the public mind in England and America, and to his own delicacy of conscience; that he may have erred in maintaining his principles with too little of that meek patience which he who would effect a reform in the opinions of men must possess, though candor will admit, that the constant opposition which Mr. Williams encountered might have irritated a gentler spirit than his; that his behavior to the civil rulers was not indecorous, unless a firm opposition to what he considered as wrong in their measures might be viewed as indecorum, for he yielded to their authority, in every point which his conscience would allow; that his private character was pure; and that the cause of his banishment may be found, in his distinguishing doctrine, *that the civil power has no control over the religious opinions of men;* a doctrine which no man, in our country, would, at the present day, venture to deny. Mr. Williams was banished, therefore, because his spirit was too elevated and enlarged, for the community in which he lived. Like Aristides, the prominent excellence of his character was the cause of his banishment.

But the same impartial verdict will do justice to the Pilgrims. They felt it to be not merely their right, but their duty, to protect their theocracy from persons, whose opinions or conduct, in their judgment, disturbed its peace or endangered its purity. They believed, that the sword of the magistrate was to be used for the defence of the church, as in the days of Moses and Aaron. To deny this principle, was to subvert the foundation of their civil and religious institutions; and it became, in their opinion, a measure of self-preservation, and of paramount duty to God, to expel Mr. Williams from the colony. That the grounds of this measure were wrong, will not now be disputed; but we ought to rejoice, that we can ascribe it to a sincere, though misdirected, desire to uphold the church, and to advance the honor of God. Were these excellent men now alive, they would be foremost in lamenting their own error, and in vindicating those principles of religious liberty, for which Mr. Williams incurred their displeasure.

And we may on this occasion, as on many others, observe the wonderful wisdom of Divine Providence, which so controls the mistakes and sins of men, as to accomplish the most important results. The banishment of Mr. Williams contributed in the end to his own happiness and fame. Another colony was established, and thus civilization and religion were diffused. And we shall soon see how this event, though springing from wrong views, and producing much immediate suffering, was the means, a few years after, of that interposition of Mr. Williams between the colonists and the Indians, which apparently rescued the whites throughout New-England from total destruction.

Henry M. Dexter: As to Roger Williams and his "Banishment" from the Massachusetts Plantation

The Rev. Henry M. Dexter was a scholarly historian and in many ways a loyal descendant of the early Puritans. He was a Congregational minister, editor of The Congregationalist, *member of the Massachusetts Historical Society and the New England Historic-Genealogical Society. The growing tendency to see the expulsion of Roger Williams as a simple infringement of religious liberty infuriated both his scholarly conscience and his ancestral loyalties. His book, published in 1876, cited a wealth of original sources as support for the following conclusions. In Dexter's view Roger Williams was clearly a "subversive" who threatened the very existence of the commonwealth of Massachusetts Bay.*

THE general subject of the character of Roger Williams, and of his relation to the early colonists of New England, has been called up to public attention afresh by a petition from sundry residents in the town of Sturbridge, Mass., addressed to the Massachusetts Legislature of 1874–5, asking them to revoke the order of banishment before which, in the winter of 1635–6, he retreated into what is now known as Rhode Island. It is not important here to refer to the various inaccuracies of statement found in that petition itself, or to discuss either the legal question how far the General Court of the Commonwealth, in these years of Grace, has power to annul action taken by the Court of the Colony two hundred and forty years ago; or the moral question, how much such action, if taken, could do in the way of securing any needed "justice" toward the remarkable man to whom reference is made, or to his memory. It does seem to be suitable, however, to avail of the occasion for making a clear, authentic and complete statement of the facts, as they actually occurred; to the end that slanders oft-repeated may be seen in their true character, and "justice" be done to *all* the noble memories involved.

It is astonishing how much the inherent difficulty of thoroughly comprehending a man who lived two or three hundred years ago is increased, if he were a somewhat pivotal and distinguished person; and, more especially, if he have been subsequently taken up and glorified, as their pet hero, by any large and enthusiastic body of believers. This seems to be particularly true of Roger Williams. The materials for his exact history are exceptionally abundant. Of few who shared with him the labors, and excitements, and controversies, of the first half-century of New England, will the close student discover so many and so amply revealing testimonies; from his own hand in letters and treatises, and from the hands of friends and enemies in letters, records, and anti-treatises. He, of all men, ought, by this time, to be as accurately as widely known. But the denomination of Christians known as Baptists, having canonized him—although never such a Baptist as they are, and for but a very short period of time a Baptist at all—have manifested great reluctance to give due consideration to a large portion of the evidence bearing upon the case; and seem to prefer, without regard to facts making fatally against their position, to re-utter the old encomiums and denunciations; as if an inadequate statement could, by persistent reiteration, be made a whole truth.

It has thus become a common representation of the case, that it was the Church-and-State controversy, and Mr. Williams's superior liberality on that subject, which led to his banishment; and it has even gone so far that leading journals of that denomination scout the very idea of any other view, as something which to all the rest of the world but Massachusetts is special pleading, that is, on the face of it, absurd.

There is a very simple, albeit a laborious, way to settle this question. It is the only way in which it ever can be settled. It is to go straight to the original sources, and candidly, and in detail, to examine them, and make up a judgment upon them; without regard to the rhetoric of superficial biographers, or prejudiced historians, or the misapprehensions of a later public sentiment by them misled. This it is proposed now to attempt. . . .

Studying carefully now all this evidence, I find it conducting the mind with irresistible force straight toward one conclusion. It is true that Mr. Williams did hold, in an inchoate form, and had already to some extent advocated, that doctrine of liberty of conscience, with which his name afterward became prominently identified. It is true that the language of the official sentence is susceptible of a construction which might include this among his "newe and dangerous opinions." It is true that Mr. Williams did himself claim that it was so included. But it appears to be also true that he himself never claimed more than this; and that, in his own view, his banishment was only incidentally—in no sense especially—for that cause. While the careful and repeated statements of Mr. Cotton, with their reiterated endorsement by Gov. Winthrop, go to show that Mr. Williams was mistaken in supposing that the subject of the rights of conscience had anything whatever to do with the action of the Court upon his case; action, in reality, solely taken in view of his seditious, defiant, and pernicious posture toward the State. This, it appears from the testimony of Mr. Gorton, and of Gov. Winslow, supported by that of Secretary Morton, of Mr. Hubbard, of Judge Scottow, of Cotton Mather and of Gov. Hutchinson, was the general understanding had of the matter by the New England public of that day; while Edwards and Baillie speak to the same point from over sea. And, as I am aware of nothing purporting to be proof to the contrary, other than the (necessarily biased, and presumably ill-informed and partial) opinion of Mr. Williams himself, before cited; I cannot help thinking that the weight of evidence is conclusive to the point that this exclusion from the Colony took place for reasons purely political, and having no relation to his notions upon toleration, or upon any subject other than those, which, in their bearing upon the common rights of property, upon the sanctions of the Oath, and upon due subordination to the powers that be in the State, made him a subverter of the very foundations of their government, and—with all his worthiness of character, and general soundness of doctrine—a nuisance which it seemed to them they had no alternative but to abate, in some way safe to them, and kindest to him!

Let it here be distinctly remembered that Roger Williams was, in 1635, a Congregational minister in good and regular standing; and so remained without any taint of doctrinal heresy for months, almost for years, after his banishment; so that he was not driven away because he was a Baptist. Nor was his offence, as so many seem to think, that he was too tolerant in spirit for his times; for the most grievous thing about him, and that which clearly most exasperated his enemies, was that he was so intensely rigid in his principles of Separation, that almost two years after John Robinson's treatise *Of the Lawfulnes of Hearing of the Ministers in the Church of England,* "found in his studie after his decease, and now published for the common good," had seen the light, he refused even to commune with his own church, because it would not break off from communing with the other churches in the Bay—for that they would not decree that if their members, when now and then visiting home in Old England, should go inside the parish churches, and listen to the preaching of the Establishment, they must undergo Ecclesiastical censure on their return for so doing!

The intelligent reader will not fail to perceive that the question which I have been laboring to settle, is one solely of fact, and not of casuistry; whether the General Court of the Governor and Company of the Massachusetts Bay did, or did not, banish Roger Williams for a certain alleged reason; rather than whether they acted wisely in what they did, or whether he deserved banishment for any reason? These are separate ranges of investigation. That which may furnish satisfactory reply to the former, may shed no gleam of light upon the latter. And having disposed of the one, it is not my purpose to enter upon any conclusive discussion of the other. I can hardly close, however, without putting on record a few further suggestions which have come to me in the study of the literature of the case, and which are perhaps worthy of being noted as contributions to any exhaustive consideration of the equity of the subject.

1. All candid inquiry must fairly weigh the true character of the plantation. I have shown that it was not an ordinary colony. It was a select settlement upon a vast, lonely, and almost empty continent, open on every side to the choice of other settlers of different affinities. It was first of all intended to afford its undertakers an opportunity to live together in the free and unmolested enjoyment, and following, of certain spiritual ideas which were very dear to them. There can be no question that they were entrusted with the legal prerogative to purge themselves of alien elements; while their right in courtesy and justice to do so, stood essentially on the same ground on which a pleasure party of special friends may properly eject an incongenial intruder. And, that one of radically hostile opinions, under these circumstances, and with the world all before him where to choose, should persist in forcing himself upon them; and, being resident among them, should spend his strength in decrying their fundamental principles, not merely, but in doing his utmost to cut the very bands by which their social order was held together; was a thing as much more intolerable to them than would be a similar procedure to the Vineland settlement, or either of those close "communities" which now exist among us; as the necessary perils of an experiment in process of trial two centuries and a half ago under nearly every conceivable disadvantage, upon the edge of a savage wilderness, must overweigh the petty risks of a modern pleasure venture in the science of sociology. And how long even Vineland would tolerate the presence of one who should disturb its peace in any manner kindred to that in which Roger Williams disturbed that of the Massachusetts Colony; and how much the well-informed community would pity such a disturber upon his consequent ejectment; I leave others to judge.

2. Not less essential is some careful consideration of the essence of the man. It is difficult to look over the grand heights of the achievements, and the loftiness of the mature quality, of some who have filled large space in the public eye, to note minutely the follies of their early days. And there was so much of sweetness, wisdom, and true nobility in the adult development of Mr. Williams, as to make it hard for us to remember that he always had great faults, and that those faults were of a kind to make his immaturity uncomfortable to others. In itself, no student could desire to go back now to draw his frailties from their dread abode; but if the justification of others become his inculpation, the truth must be spoken. It would be a curious study of character to follow exhaustively the traces he has left of himself upon the history of his time—in what he did and said, and wrote; and in what others wrote to, and of him, and said about him. Those were days of free and rugged speech, when even the best of men sometimes allowed themselves to suspect and stigmatize the motives of others, and to employ bitter words in so doing; and just allowance must be made for this. But after all due deduction, it will unquestionably be concluded that Mr. Williams did somehow exceptionally provoke the censures of the good. When he lived in Mas-

sachusetts, he was evidently a hot-headed youth, of determined perseverance, vast energy, considerable information, intense convictions, a decided taste for novelty, a hearty love of controversy, a habit of hasty speech with absolute carelessness of consequences, and a religious horror of all expediency; whose logical instincts and whose mobile sensibilities acted and reacted upon each other with intensifying power; whose convictions of moral obligation were as likely to be the result of sudden flashes of feeling as of calm and well balanced consideration; and whose eyes were so intently fixed upon a great ideal line of duty stretching onward through the far future, and upward toward the judgment seat, as to withdraw his consciousness largely from the path that was under his feet, and so to permit him to stumble into entangling inconsistencies which might have been avoided if his attention had been more recalled to the practical obligations of the hour. He forgot, too, that God's ships seldom have a wind fair enough to speed with a flowing sheet straight into port; and that the most pious seamanship must often manifest itself in sailing close-hauled as near toward the desired point as may be, and in getting, in the face of adverse gales ever and anon well about from the starboard to the lar-board tack, and the reverse; while the highest, devoutest skill of all may sometimes show itself in laying to, in the face of a storm which, for the time being, forbids all progress. John Quincy Adams happily characterized him as "conscientiously contentious." Equally felicitous is Prof. Masson's phrase describing him as "the arch-Individualist."

With all, were an abiding patience under trial, and meekness toward reproof; a calm courage, a [illegible] estedness and public spi[illegible] dominant good temper in ever[illegible] and toward every opponent, which were the crown and glory of his remarkable character; . . .

It is not, necessarily, a hyperbole to say that the better, the more devout—and Mr. Williams was devout, "the people being, many of them, much taken with the apprehension of his godliness"—such a man might be; the more dangerous, under certain circumstances, his influence might become.

3. It may be well, moreover, for the student who desires to go to the bottom of the subject of the banishment of Mr. Williams, to expend a little thought upon the question whether the importance of the transaction itself has not been overestimated and overstated. Clearly the action of the Court, at the time, notwithstanding the local excitement at Salem, made small general sensation. It was merely the renewed exercise, for cause, of a power repeatedly before asserted. In the February following, the event was lumped with some petty troubles in the church at Lynn, and with the existing scarcity of corn, as occasioning the proclamation of a fast in the Colony. Thomas Lechford, who published his *Newes from New England* in 1642, although he speaks of Williams, says nothing of it. Capt. Edward Johnson, in the *Wonder-Working Providence of Sions Saviour in New England,* in 1654, makes only slight and obscure reference to this, although he devotes considerable space to the disturbances occasioned by Samuel Gorton and Mistress Hutchinson. Quaint Cotton Mather—with an obvious suggestion—entitles his chapter which is mainly devoted to Mr. Williams and Samuel Gorton, "Little Foxes." Dr. Bac-

kus was the first of our historians to develop the modern idea of the vast significance of the trial, and he was writing "A History of New England with particular reference to the Denomination of Christians called Baptists." While those biographers of our day who have acted on the hints which he gave, and drawn attention to that rude court-room at New Town on the 9–19 Oct. 1635, as if it were one of the focal points of modern history, —Knowles, Gammell, Elton and Underwood—have all been Baptists. On the whole, perhaps Dr. Palfrey is nearer right, when he styles the disturbance produced by it, "limited, superficial, and transient," and goes on to add:

Had it not been for later transactions, which revealed him in more favorable lights, and for the connection of his exile with the origin of a State, that exile, instead of taking the place in history in which it presents itself to us, might have been recorded simply as the expulsion of one among several eccentric and turbulent persons. His controversy speedily narrowed down to a merely personal dispute; not a half-score of friends followed when he went away, nor were they of a character to show that he inspired confidence in the best and soberest men; scarcely a larger number of persons who remained behind adhered to his peculiarities; and the returning waters presently closed over the track his dashing bark had made. . . .

4. It is indispensable, further, that one note the temper of those times. For half a century there had been a religious commotion in England which had effectually stirred up the masses of the people, and in the general confusion, dangerous elements had now and then manifested themselves. Most adult New Englanders could then remember the Gunpowder plot, and shared that intense and stinging hatred of Popery, as politically synonymous with treason, as well as odious in its superstitions, which has not even yet died out of the hearts of the London populace; whom one sees still fiercely handling their effigies of Guy Fawkes on the 15th November. One hundred years before, a terrible fanaticism had raged over Germany and the Netherlands, which had left in the general conservative mind a vague, yet vivid, horror of all claims to special light from heaven, all particularly loud-voiced accusations of public sin, and especially all plans looking towards civil reconstruction, and all denunciations of the regular magistracy, and the usual sanctions of justice; as being—all ills in one—Anabaptism! The settlers of Massachusetts, as a class, were moderate reformers; as anxious, on the one hand, not to wreck their enterprise and imperil its reputation among the sober-minded at home, by excesses in the name of liberty; as, on the other, to avoid being forced back into the old conformity, or—still further back—into the clutch of the Man of Sin. We have seen moreover, that Mr. Williams's advent, and busy activity in Massachusetts affairs, had taken the plantation in an evil time in respect to the fact that the arrogant Court of England was just then looking toward it with some intent against its charter; that disaffected persons, who had been sent home for the colony's good, were doing their utmost to play into the hands of the King by accusing the settlers of intending rebellion, of proposing entire and absolute separation from the mother country, of habitually railing against the State, Church and Bishops, and of revolutionary and anarchical behavior, in general. Only by remembering that at every step the chief actors in Mr. Williams's case would feel themselves compelled to inquire what

the effect of all was likely to be in London, can one hope to arrive at any entirely fair judgment upon the quality of their action.

Pre-eminently is it essential that the dread, and almost horror, with which a general toleration of religious beliefs was then conscientiously regarded by most good men, be recalled; because it is conceded on all hands that Mr. Williams was already to some extent a believer in, and an advocate of this doctrine; although, as we have seen, the subject entered only in the most unimportant manner, if at all, into the conflict of opinion which led to his removal.

5. It would be well, also, that some consideration be given to the necessity, and the alternative, then existing, into which Mr. Williams himself had forced the Company. Matters had been pushed by him to such a pass that, so far as his influence extended, all were really standing on the very edge of chaos. Had he been permitted to remain, and been able to carry out his views, it is not easy to see how some grand catastrophe could have been averted. The patent would have been surrendered to the King with repentance and humiliation that any use had ever been made of it; which would have dropped the bottom at once from under all commercial foundations, destroyed all land-titles, and disorganized business among them in every department; while in the existing condition of the royal mind, they could have hoped for no redressive grant, or legislation. The administration of the Freemen's and Resident's Oath would have been abrogated; and the way thereby opened to a disintegration of civil affairs rivaling in disastrous completeness that which would have been wrought upon their commerce by the other. In a religious point of view, their Congregational liberality would have been transmuted into an unlovely, unreasonable and bitter Separatism; which would have made the colony odious, as well as ridiculous, in the eyes of all intelligent and high-minded men, even of that day; in that it would insist on disfellowshiping every New England church which should decline to excommunicate one of its own members, who, revisiting Old England, should drop in to hear a sermon, even from the godliest rector, in an Established church, without avowing his repentance of the act, as of a sin, on his return. While that most hateful and dangerous form of the interaction of Church and State which Mr. Williams—in spite of all his philosophies—had entered upon, in endeavoring, through the medium of the discipline of the churches to which they belonged, to compel the members of the General Court to modify their action in regard to the Marblehead land, endangered an excitement, and an overturning, in those churches, quite as much to be dreaded as any calamities likely to ensue in other departments of the public welfare.

The irresistible fact which confronts the honest and thorough inquirer into the minute history of that time, a fact which cannot be ignored, nor explained away, is that the teaching and influence of Roger Williams—to use the careful language of John Quincy Adams—were "altogether revolutionary." Our fathers felt themselves reluctantly compelled to choose between his expulsion, and the immediate risk of social, civil and religious disorganization. To say otherwise is to confess an amount of ignorance, or a degree of prejudice, sufficient to disqualify one from forming any useful opinion upon the subject.

6. In this connection it is impossible to overlook the marked kindness with which Mr. Williams was treated by the Massachusetts men. They were very patient with him under circumstances eminently calculated to exhaust patience. When complaint had been first made against his teaching, his letter of apology was generously received. And when, some ten months after, the Court were informed that he had broken his promises, and renewed the obnoxious and dangerous teachings, nearly half a year was still allowed to lapse before he was brought to their bar to answer. Even then two months more passed by before any formal trial. That trial ended in the express adjournment of the whole subject, through three further months, to the next General Court; in the hope that he would be brought to "give satisfaction." At the final hearing he was tendered still another month's additional delay; was labored with, at length, by one of his peers in the ministry in the vain endeavor to persuade him to abandon his positions; and was then granted six additional weeks—which weeks were subsequently lengthened into months—before the requisition of final departure. It was only from a necessity induced by his own point blank violation of all the conditions on which postponement had been accorded, that his leave to remain was cut short in January. Nor was he even then "driven from the society of civilized man, and debarred the consolations of Christian sympathy to find among heathen savages the boon of charity which was refused at home,"—a "solitary pilgrim," in "the sternest month of a New England winter," under "great hardship." It was the purpose of the magistrates to send him by ship comfortably home to England; not as a criminal for trial, but as a British subject; who having proved incompatible here, might take other chances of usefulness and happiness there. Evading this by sudden flight, it was still at his option to have sought the near shelter of the Plymouth Colony, where aforetime he had found welcome, and which was never addicted to banishing people; or to have turned his steps northward toward white men, nascent institutions, and comfortable, albeit as yet rude, firesides on the banks of the Cocheco, or under the shadows of Agamenticus.

Mr. Gammell intimates an injustice in the proceedings against Mr. Williams, on the ground that "there appears to have been no examination of witnesses, and no hearing of counsel"; and this is echoed by Prof. Elton. It is astonishing that intimations so unfounded should come from gentlemen of such intelligence. One would think they could neither have read the contemporary account of the trial, nor studied the history of the time. No witnesses are needed where the defendant pleads guilty to all charges, and seeks to justify the acts complained of; while the employment of counsel, in the modern sense, to aid in any trial, was then, and for years after, a thing unknown in the colony.

I insist, then, that forbearance and gentleness of spirit toward Mr. Williams, did characterize the proceedings of the Governor and Company of the Massachusetts Bay. It was his bitterly separative spirit which began and kept alive the difficulty,—not theirs. He withdrew communion from them—not they from him. In all strictness and honesty he persecuted them—not they him; just as the modern "Come-outer," who persistently intrudes his bad manners, and pestering presence upon some private company, making himself, upon pretence of conscience, a nuisance there; is—if sane—the persecutor, rather than the man who forcibly assists, as well as courteously requires, his desired departure. . . .

And not until the student has patiently considered the points here presented—the peculiar character of the plantation; the idiosyncrasies of the man; the actual nature of a "banishment" often overestimated, as well as misunderstood; the temper of the times; the quality of the necessity which Mr. Williams himself had created, and the nature of the alternative which he had forced upon the colonists; yet the thorough and inexhaustible kindness with which, nevertheless, they treated him; with the facts that—in nearly every particular—he subsequently confessed the substantial justice of their dealing with him, and that in the important matter of the Patent, he abandoned his own opinion to revert to theirs—will he be in a position fitting him to speak wisely and conclusively upon this vexed passage of New England history.

PART IV. SOME TWENTIETH–CENTURY INTERPRETATIONS OF THE CONFLICT BETWEEN ROGER WILLIAMS AND THE MASSACHUSETTS AUTHORITIES

Vernon L. Parrington: ROGER WILLIAMS, SEEKER

In 1927 Vernon Parrington published Main Currents of American Thought, *a remarkably fresh and influential study of American intellectual history. Parrington described his viewpoint as "liberal rather than conservative, Jeffersonian rather than Federalistic" and claimed that, "The line of liberalism in colonial America runs through Roger Williams, Benjamin Franklin, and Thomas Jefferson." In this view Williams took on new significance as a major hero of the American democratic tradition, a man who was "primarily a political philosopher rather than a theologian."*

THE gods, it would seem, were pleased to have their jest with Roger Williams by sending him to earth before his time. In manner and speech a seventeenth-century Puritan controversialist, in intellectual interests he was contemporary with successive generations of prophets from his own days to ours. His hospitable mind anticipated a surprising number of the idealisms of the future. As a transcendental mystic he was a forerunner of Emerson and the Concord school, discovering an indwelling God of love in a world of material things; as a speculative Seeker he was a forerunner of Channing and the Unitarians, discovering the hope of a more liberal society in the practice of the open mind; as a political philosopher he was a forerunner of Paine and the French romantic school, discovering the end of government in concern for the *res publica*, and the cohesive social tie in the principle of good will. Democrat and Christian, the generation to which he belongs is not yet born, and all his life he remained a stranger amongst men. Things natural and right to John Cotton were no better than anachronisms to him. He lived and dreamed in a future he was not to see, impatient to bring to men a heaven they were unready for. And because they were unready they could not understand the grounds of his hope, and not understanding they were puzzled and angry and cast him out to dream his dreams in the wilderness. There was abundant reason for his banishment. A child of light, he came bringing not peace but the sword. A humane and liberal spirit, he was groping for a social order more generous than any theocracy—that should satisfy the aspirations of men for a catholic fellowship, greater than sect or church, village or nation, embracing all races and creeds, bringing together the sundered societies of men in a common spirit of good will.

Roger Williams was the most provocative figure thrown upon the Massachusetts shores by the upheaval in England, the one original thinker amongst a number of capable social architects. An intellectual barometer, fluctuating with every change in the rising storm of revolution, he came transporting hither the new and disturbant doctrines of the Leveler, loosing wild foxes with firebrands to ravage the snug fields of the Presbyterian Utopia. He was the "*first rebel* against the divine *church-order* established in the wilderness," as Cotton Mather rightly reported. But he was very much more than that; he was a rebel against all the stupidities that interposed a barrier betwixt men and the fellowship of their dreams. Those who found such stupidities serviceable to their ends, naturally disliked Roger Williams and believed they were serving God by undoing his work. There is a naïve passage in the *Magnalia* that suggests how incomprehensible to the theocratic mind was this stormy petrel that came out of England to flutter and clamor about Boston and Salem, until he was driven forth to find such resting place as he might, there to bring forth after his kind.

> In the year 1654, a certain windmill in the Low Countries, whirling round with extraordinary violence, by reason of a violent storm then blowing, the stone at length by its rapid motion became so intensely hot as to fire the mill, from whence the flames, being dispersed by the high winds, did set a whole Town on fire. But I can tell my reader that, above twenty years before this, there was a whole country in America like to be set on fire by the rapid motion of a Windmill in the head of one particular man.

And John Cotton, worsted in his bout with his brilliant antagonist, and perhaps frightened at the latter's free speculation, found such satisfaction as he could in epithets. Roger Williams was an "evill-worker"; his "head runneth round"; "it would weary a sober minde to pursue such windy fancies," such "offensive and disturbant doctrines"; when "a man is delivered up to Satan . . . no marvell if he cast forth fire-brands, and arrows, and mortall-things"; "it is such a transcendent light, as putteth out all the lights in the world besides."

The open facts of Roger Williams' life are known to everybody. Born in the year 1603, he became a protégé of the great Coke, was educated at Cambridge, and destined for the law, but forsook it for the ministry. He was well advanced in his studies and coming to conclusions that must have disturbed his conservative friends, at the time of the Great Migration. Beginning as an Anglican, then turning Separatist, then Baptist, and finally Seeker, he is perhaps more adequately described as a Puritan intellectual who became a Christian freethinker, more concerned with social commonwealths than with theological dogmas. He passed rapidly through successive phases of current thought to end as a Leveler. Before quitting England he had embraced the principle of Separatism, and on his first coming over he refused the teachership of the Boston church—the position given to Cotton two years later—because it had not broken wholly with Anglicanism. He went to the more liberal Salem, where his inconvenient questioning of land titles and his views on the charter brought him into conflict with the Boston authorities. Refusing to be silenced he was banished and made his way to Rhode Island—"sorely tossed for one fourteen weeks, in a bitter winter season, not knowing what bread or bed did mean"—there to found a commonwealth on democratic principles.

Yet how inadequately do such meager facts reveal the deeper sources of his militancy! He lived in the realm of ideas, of inquiry and discussion; and his actions were creatively determined by principles the bases of which he examined with critical insight. Instead of being a weather vane, blown about by every wind of doctrine, he was an adventurous pioneer, surveying the new fields of thought laid open by the Reformation, and marking out the several spheres of church and state in the ordering of a true commonwealth. He was the incarnation of Protestant individualism, seeking new social ties to take the place of those that were loosening; and as a child of a great age of political speculation his religion issued in political theory rather than in theological dogma. Like other Separatist-Levelers he had penetrated to the foundations of the New Testament and had taken to heart the revolutionary ideals that underlie its teachings. It was the spirit of love that served as teacher to him; love that exalted the meanest to equality with the highest in the divine republic of Jesus, and gave an exalted sanction to the conception of a Christian commonwealth. He regarded his fellow men literally as the children of God and brothers in Christ; and from this primary conception of the fatherhood of God and the brotherhood of man, he deduced his political philosophy. Like Channing two hundred years later, he sought to adjust his social program to the determining fact that human worth knows neither Jew nor Gentile, rank nor caste; and following the example of his Master he went forth into a hostile world, seeking to make it over.

With this spirit of Christian fellowship, warm and human and lovable, repudiating all coercion, there was joined an eager mysticism—a yearning for intimate personal union with Christ as symbolized in the parable of the vine and the branches, a union as close as that of the bride and her husband. Running through his writings is a recurrent echo of the Hebrew love-song that Puritan thought suffused with a glowing mysticism: "I am my beloved's and my beloved is mine: he feedeth among the lilies. . . . I will rise now, and go about the city in the streets, and in the broad ways I will seek him whom my soul loveth." But when he went out into the broad ways of Carolinian England, seeking the rose of Sharon and the lily of the valley, he discovered only abominations. The lover was tempted by false kisses; the Golden Image was set up in the high places, and the voice of authority commanded to bow down to it. And so as a Christian mystic Roger Williams became a Separatist, and set his mind upon the new world as a land where the lover might dwell with his bride. Yet upon his arrival there he found the churches still "implicitly National," and "yet asleep in respect of abundant ignorance and negligence, and consequently grosse abominations and pollutions of Worship, in which the choicest servants of God, and most faithful Witnesses of many truths have lived in more or lesse, yea in maine and fundamental points, ever since the Apostasie." Which "abominations and pollutions of worship," he now proposed to sweep away altogether. It was not an easy program, nor one entered upon lightly. Better than most, Roger Williams understood how closely interwoven were the threads of church and state. Separatism, with its necessary corollary of toleration, could not be unraveled from

Carolinian society without loosening the whole social fabric. It was a political question even more than ecclesiastical; and it could justify itself only in the light of a total political philosophy. No other man in New England comprehended so fully the difficulties involved in the problem, as Roger Williams, or examined them so thoroughly; and out of his long speculations emerged a theory of the commonwealth that must be reckoned the richest contribution of Puritanism to American political thought.

The just renown of Roger Williams has too long been obscured by ecclesiastical historians, who in emphasizing his defense of the principle of toleration have overlooked the fact that religious toleration was only a necessary deduction from the major principles of his political theory, and that he was concerned with matters far more fundamental than the negative virtue of non-interference in the domain of individual faith. He was primarily a political philosopher rather than a theologian—one of the acutest and most searching of his generation of Englishmen, the teacher of Vane and Cromwell and Milton, a forerunner of Locke and the natural-rights school, one of the notable democratic thinkers that the English race has produced. Much of his life was devoted to the problem of discovering a new basis for social reorganization, and his intellectual progress was marked by an abundant wreckage of obsolete theory and hoary fiction that strewed his path. He was a social innovator on principle, and he left no system unchallenged; each must justify itself in reason and expediency or be put aside. Broadly the development of his thought falls into three stages: the substitution of the compact theory of the state for the divine-right theory; the rejection of the suppositious compact of the earlier school and the fictitious abstract state—still postulated by many thinkers—and the substitution of a realistic conception of the political state as the sovereign repository of the social will, and the government—or agent of the state—as the practical instrument of society to effect its desired ends; and finally, the difficult problem of creating the necessary machinery of a democratic commonwealth, as the exigencies of the Rhode Island experiment required. Throughout, the inspiration of his thinking was social rather than narrowly political or theological, and the creative source would seem to have been the middle ages with their fruitful principle of men in a given society enrolling themselves voluntarily as members of bodies corporate, finding in such corporate ties a sufficient and all-embracing social bond. . . .

England gave her best when she sent us Roger Williams. A great thinker and a bold innovator, the repository of the generous liberalisms of a vigorous age, he brought with him the fine wheat of long years of English tillage to sow in the American wilderness. How much America owes to him is perhaps, after all the intervening years, not adequately realized; the shadow of Massachusetts Bay still too much obscures the large proportions of one who was certainly the most generous, most open-minded, most lovable, of the Puritan emigrants—the truest Christian amongst many who sincerely desired to be Christian. He believed in men and in their native justice, and he spent his life freely in the cause of humanity. Neither race nor creed sundered him from his fellows; the Indian was his brother equally with the Englishman. He was a Leveler because he was convinced that society with its caste institutions dealt unjustly with the common man; he was a democrat because he believed that the end and object of the political state was the common well-being; he was an iconoclast because he was convinced that the time had come when a new social order must be erected on the decay of the old. "*Liberavi animam meam*," he said with just pride; "I have not hid within my *breast* my *souls* belief." "It was more than forty years after his exile that he lived here," wrote Cotton Mather, "and in many thinges acquitted himself so laudably, that many juditious persons judged him to have the root of the matter in him, during the long winter of this retirement." Since those words were written increasing numbers of "juditious persons" have come to agree with the reluctant judgment of Cotton Mather, and are verily persuaded that Master Roger Williams "had the root of the matter in him." In his own day he was accounted an enemy of society, and the commonwealth of Massachusetts has never rescinded the decree of banishment issued against him; yet like so many unshackled thinkers, he was a seeker after a better order, friend to a nobler and more humane society. If he transported to America the democratic aspirations of English Independency, it is perhaps well to recall the price that was exacted of him for his service:

> Let the reader fancy him in 1640, a man of thirty-four, of bold and stout jaws, but with the richest and softest eyes, gazing out over the Bay of his dwelling, a spiritual Crusoe, the excommunicated even of Hugh Peters, and the most extreme and outcast soul in all America.

Samuel Hugh Brockunier: THE IRREPRESSIBLE DEMOCRAT: ROGER WILLIAMS

Parrington's view of Williams as the first great American democrat was more fully developed in a biography by Samuel Brockunier. Written during the late 1930's, a time when Americans were curbing economic privileges at home and facing threats to democracy from abroad, this biography claimed that Roger Williams would be significant for Americans so long as they "retained a belief in equalitarianism" and struggled to resolve "class conflict and social maladjustment by the democratic process." For Brockunier and for many college textbooks in which his view is still presented Williams's concern for religious liberty was made secondary to an attack upon the economic privileges and political power of an "oligarchy" in Massachusetts.

TROUBLER OF ISRAEL

On February 5, 1631, Roger and Mary Williams first set foot on New World soil. Governor Winthrop, welcoming the *Lyon*, made a note of some of her passengers: "She brought Mr. Williams (a godly minister) with his wife, Mr. Throgmorton," and some others. Winthrop had met the young chaplain at Sempringham, and it is apparent that Williams' zeal and ability brought him a ready welcome at Boston. The way to preferment in New England opened before him. Hooker, Stone, Cotton, Shepard, Eliot, Nathaniel Ward, and other great lights of New England churches had not yet come. Boston was even now temporarily deprived of the services of John Wilson, and before long the "godly" young minister from the *Lyon* was offered the place as teacher of the leading church in the colony. In 1631 the magistrates and ministers of Massachusetts expected Roger Williams to become one of them.

It was not to be Williams' destiny to become one of that charmed inner circle. His first action was a portent of much that was to follow. "Being unanimously chosen teacher at Boston," he wrote, he conscientiously refused "because I durst not officiate to an unseparated people, as upon examination and conference I found them to be." Williams was not insensible of the opportunity for advancement and certainly he desired a church, but not at the price of his convictions. He might, he declared later, "have run the rode of preferment, as well as in Old as New England. . . ." He now exhibited that characteristic belief in "coming out," separating from a corrupt church, which was to denote him as spiritual kin of the Independent sects and not of the Non-separatists of England and Massachusetts. He could not become teacher, he told them in Boston, unless the congregation would repent its former communion in the Church of England and discourage its members from communing with that church when they visited the homeland.

Non-separatists of the Ames persuasion could not accede to this, and Williams soon departed for Salem where the Ames doctrine was not yet so firmly rooted. Before leaving Boston he declared his adherence to another principle which caused equal shock to those of the Bay. The civil magistrate, he declared, might not punish "breach of the Sabbath" nor any other violations of "the first table." Since the first table, comprising the first four of the Ten Commandments, consisted of the Mosaic injunctions against idolatry, blasphemy, and heresy, Williams in effect was denying the power of the government to compel conformity in matters of faith. Already he was bolstering his Separatism with something which looked dangerously akin to condonement of schism.

Williams departed to Salem without a summons or warning, but trouble was brewing. By April 12 word came to Governor Winthrop "that they of Salem had called Mr. Williams to the office of a teacher." Coddington, Ludlow, Bradstreet, and other nearby assistants deliberated at Boston and determined on the first in a long series of actions against Williams. They sent a letter to John Endecott, assistant at Salem, charging that "Mr. Williams had refused to join with the congregation at Boston" because they would not make public repentance "for having communion with the churches of England, while they lived there." The newly chosen teacher of Salem had also "declared his opinion, that the magistrate might not punish the breach of the Sabbath, nor any other offence, as it was a breach of the first table; therefore, they marvelled they would choose him without advising with the council; and withal desiring him, that they would forbear to proceed till they had conferred about it."

No law existed which authorized interference with the right of a congregation to elect its officers, but this was neither the first nor the last time that the magistrates relied upon their claim of discre-

[illegible] and effectively over-[illegible]gation. Williams found [illegible] a church and removed [illegible]ymouth. For the moment, th[illegible]s had freed themselves of the threat o[illegible] [illegible]eparatism.

Williams' Separatism and the issue it presented frequently has been misunderstood. Because Williams urged renunciation of the Church of England, New England Puritans who rejected this step have been upheld as more tolerant. "It is a surprising fact," remarked Goodwin, "that any person should have left Boston of 1631 because he found there religious liberality which amounted to a sin; but the surprise is increased manyfold when the person so departing is found to have been Roger Williams." The real issue was the conflict between the sectarian principle which tended toward a free church system and toleration and the ideal of one authoritarian church which included the whole society. Even as early as 1631 Williams aligned himself in support of the sectarian ideal and affirmed the right and the necessity of separating from false and idolatrous worship and of setting up an independent church.

Five years later, after Williams departed for Rhode Island, he and Cotton exchanged letters on this subject and Williams charged that Non-separatism attempted to "walke betwixt Christ and Anti-Christ"; to which Cotton replied that "the Lord hath guided us to walk with an even foote between two extremes." Between these two positions there was an irreconcilable difference. Williams in the years to come unerringly exposed the lack of logic in "witnessing against a national Church and yet holding fellowship with it"; but there lay a subtle harmony in Non-separatism which outwitted logic. Those of the school of Ames might witness against the church of Laud—and did—but they must not separate. They must give no sanction to Separatism because they must give no sanction to schism. They must uphold the divine right of the church of the prelates because they must uphold their own claim of divine authority, as hopeful heirs apparent next in the line of succession. Laud might hold sway for the moment, but the Non-separatist trusted to the Massachusetts example and the growing might of numbers in England to conquer the church itself. Trained in the school of Ames, Governor Winthrop and the Bay leaders would not quarrel with the absolutist principle of the Church of England, nor separate from it while they hoped to capture it. Meanwhile behind the bulwark of three thousand miles of ocean they proceeded to set up a new clericalism in place of the one they had left and to substitute the uniformity of Ames for the uniformity of Laud. Roger Williams in 1631 betook himself to Plymouth with different ideas, and if for the moment he merely asserted the right and necessity of Separatism against the English church, it would not be long before he would assert the same right against the churches of Massachusetts.

There are few records of Williams' life in Plymouth colony. According to Governor Bradford, he was kindly "entertained, according to their poore abilitie" and became a member of the church. Since Plymouth people stemmed from the Separatists who had once fled to Holland, Williams' doctrine was less suspect than in Massachusetts and he "exercised his gifts amongst them" as assistant to the Reverend Ralph Smith who also had been ordered from Salem on the grounds of Separatism.

In October, 1632, Winthrop and other worthies from the Bay were entertained at the older colony of the Pilgrims.

On the afternoon of the sabbath "Mr. Roger Williams (according to their custom) propounded a question, to which the pastor, Mr. Smith, spake briefly; then Mr. Williams prophesied." After Bradford and several others of Plymouth had spoken to the question, they desired Winthrop and John Wilson, minister at Boston, to speak to it, "which they did." Perhaps the question presented at these exercises related to the "goodman" controversy. Williams and Smith, according to Cotton Mather, were "leavened so far with the humors of the rigid separation, that they insisted vehemently upon the unlawfulness of calling any unregenerate man by the name of 'good-man such an one,' until by their indiscreet urging of this whimsey, the place began to be disquieted." When this question was propounded during the visit of Winthrop, the Massachusetts governor gave his opinion that such salutations were a mere "civil custom"; which, Mather declared, "put a stop to the little, idle, whimsical conceits, then beginning to grow obstreperous." Winthrop's own account of his Plymouth visit does not mention such an incident, nor does Bradford, and the story may be apocryphal. Yet Williams on occasion exhibited religious scruples which he spun to airy flimsiness, and the anecdote of Cotton Mather does not seem improbable. In after years at Providence, the records spoke often of "neighbor" so and so, but seldom made use of the appellation "goodman."

Such an episode, if it occurred, was of minor consequence, and in his two years at Plymouth, Williams gained the high regard of the congregation by his services in the church and his labors among the Indians. Governor Bradford acknowledged him "a man godly and zealous, having many precious parts." His account of Williams, written after the latter's banishment from Massachusetts, was colored by that event. Williams was "very unsettled in judgment"; yet his teaching was

> well approoved, for the benefite wherof I still blese God, and am thankfull to him, even for his sharpest admonitions and reproufs, so farr as they agreed with truth. He this year begane to fall into some strang oppĩons, and from opinion to practise; which caused some contraversie betweene the church and him, and in the end some discontente on his parte, by occasion whereof he left them some thing abruptly. Yet after wards sued for his dismission to the church of Salem, which was granted, with some caution to them concerning him, and what care they ought to have of him.

The unnamed bone of contention was probably Williams' advanced views of Separatism. Although sired by the earlier school of Separatists, Plymouth was swinging back to views like those of Ames, and "rigid separation" was becoming suspect at Plymouth as well as in the Bay. Bradford seems to have approved of the subsequent banishment of Williams by Massachusetts. In the course of time the conventional Plymouth estimate of Williams' ministry became considerably less kindly than Bradford's. Nathaniel Morton's account, published in 1669, reflected the glacial drift of later Puritan days and marked the development of the scathing or satirical portrayal of the celebrated Rhode Islander which, repeated by Hubbard, was embellished and perpetuated by Cotton Mather. Morton's version depicted Williams as "well accepted" on his first arrival at Plymouth, but as gradually venting "singular opinions"—not specified—and seeking to "impose" them on the congregation; "not finding such a concurrence as he expected," he requested "dismission to the church of Salem, which though some were unwilling to, yet through the prudent counsel of Mr. Brewster, the ruling elder there, fearing that his continuance amongst them might cause divisions, and there being many abler men in the bay, they would better deal with him than themselves could. . . ." At the time of its publication years later Williams wrote laughingly of this account to John Winthrop, Jr.: "Sir, since I saw you I have read Morton's Memorial, and rejoice at the encomiums upon your father and other precious worthies, though I be a reprobate, *contemptâ vitior algâ.*"

Some time between July and November, 1633, Williams removed to Salem and became assistant to the pastor of the church, Samuel Skelton, "but not in any office," noted Winthrop, "though he exercised by way of prophecy. . . ." In this capacity Williams was soon in opposition to one of the new ecclesiastical practices by which the clergy were consolidating their control of the churches. The ministers had begun to hold periodical meetings at which "some question of moment was debated." Skelton and Williams "took some exception against it, as fearing it might grow in time to a presbytery or superintendency, to the prejudice of the churches' liberties." Williams, as in 1631 when he questioned the disciplinary power of magistrates, was fearful of a new hierarchy and a national church and seized upon a defense of congregational independence as the surest way to combat compulsory uniformity and clerical absolutism. Winthrop understood the point but he derided such fears as "without cause; for they were all clear in that point, that no church or person can have power over another church; neither did they in their meetings exercise any such jurisdiction. . . ." Only four years later the first synod in Massachusetts was to belie Winthrop's words. The system of synods, consociation, ministerial advice to the magistrates, and magisterial enforcement of the first table was presently to establish a "superintendency" over the churches and shackle local congregations in the iron clasp of the centralized uniformity that Williams had feared.

In December, 1633, Governor Winthrop made a notation of another protest by Williams:

> The governour and assistants met at Boston and took into consideration a treatise, which Mr. Williams (then of Salem) had sent to them, and which he had formerly written to the governour and council of Plimouth, wherein, among other things, he disputes their right to the lands they possessed here, and concluded that, claiming by the king's grant, they could have no title, nor otherwise, except they compounded with the natives.

This striking criticism of the practice of European monarchs of granting vast tracts inhabited by Indians arose out of Williams' friendship with the natives and concern for their rights. From Plymouth he wrote Winthrop, "I am no Elder in any church . . . nor ever shall be, if the Lord please to grant my desires that I may intend what I long after, the natives souls. . . ." From the first, Williams had a keen desire to "dive into the Indian language." He and Massasoit, sachem of the Wampanoags, became "great friends at Plymouth"; he spared no cost in tokens and presents to him and "all his," and had friendly relations also with Canonicus, great sachem of the Narragansetts. The description of New England by William Wood, published in 1634, spoke in warm praise: "One of the English Preachers in a speciall good intent of doing good to their soules, hath spent much time in attaining to their

Language, wherein he is so good a proficient, that he can speake to their understanding, and they to his; much loving and respecting him for his love and counsell. It is hoped that he may be an instrument of good amongst them." Eliot had not begun his notable labors; the unnamed missionary was Roger Williams.

Williams' manuscript on Plymouth patent has not survived, but it is clear that he called on the planters to make amends for the "sinne of unjust usurpation upon others possessions." The Indians alone were lords of the soil and no grant by the king could alienate their title. The "great sin" of New England's patents lay in their provisions respecting "Donation of the Land"—"wherein Christian Kings (so called) are invested with Right by virtue of their Christianitie, to take and give away the Lands and Countries of other men."

The action of the authorities on this issue revealed forcibly to Williams the increasingly close association of leading clerics and magistrates. The court sounded out "some of the most judicious ministers," doubtless among them John Cotton, the great new light of Boston church, and the ministers promptly brought in a verdict which "much condemned Mr. Williams's error and presumption. . . ." The magistrates thereupon summoned Williams "to be censured." By private intervention Winthrop averted immediate disciplinary action. He wrote Endecott to confer with Williams and secure a retraction; and in response to this overture, the young Salem cleric stated the simple truth of the question without rancor. His treatise had not been aimed specifically against the Massachusetts patent but had been written at Plymouth "for the private satisfaction" of the authorities there. The Bay magistrates would have heard nothing of the matter if Winthrop had not asked him for a copy of the tract; and if they desired, they might burn the manuscript or the parts objectionable.

The "offensive passages" in Williams' manuscript turned on certain allegations which reflected upon royalty. Williams had charged James with "a solemn public lie" in acclaiming himself the first Christian prince to discover "this land." The magistrates knew as well as Williams that James had no title as discoverer of the continent; but they were not prepared to contradict the royal word. Nor was it expedient to attack James' patent for calling Europe "Christendom." True, the infidel Turk held much of Europe, and all Puritans knew that "Anti-Christ" ruled over much of the rest. Still more impolitic was Williams' citation of three uncomplimentary passages from *Revelations* which he "did personally apply to our present king, Charles." Nevertheless on January 24 the authorities found the offensive passages "obscure" and matters not "so evil as at first they seemed," and with the concurrence of Cotton and Wilson, the court withheld its censure.

This affair of the patent, while indicative of Williams' tendency to scruple over trivia, first revealed his stature as one of the few Englishmen who demanded equal justice for the natives. According to Cotton, Williams contended that the Indians "hunted all the Countrey over" and on their big hunts once or twice a year burnt out the underbrush—as sufficient proof of their "Propriety of the Countrey"; an evidence of title at least as good as that of English nobles to their "great Parkes" or of the king to his "great Forrests." The Massachusetts retort to Williams on this point was subtle and revealing. Although admitting the

Indian title by generally paying "purchase money" for lands, the Bay authorities did not relish a defense of the "Propriety" of the natives. Land-hungry Puritans were not disposed to treat the heathen as the equals of "Saints." The fat lands of nobles and king in the mother country, they said, were earned by great services to church and state. As for the aborigines and their hunting grounds: "We did not conceive that it is a just Title to so vast a Continent, to make no other improvement of millions of Acres in it. . . ."

Governor Winthrop, to confound Williams with good European legalism, declared bluntly that "these parts" were "*vacuum Domicilium.*" Even before embarking from the homeland, Winthrop had dug into the Old Testament for the warrant of Higher Law. The cases of Ephron the Hittite, Jacob and Hamor's land, and the relations of Abimelech's servants with Isaac's readily came to hand, and Winthrop concluded that the Indians had only a "natural right" to the soil, the right of occupancy. Land that lay in common and had never been replenished or subdued was "free to any that possesse and improve it. . . . Soe if we leave them sufficient for their use, we may lawfully take the rest, there being more than enough for them and us. . . ." Along this road lay hidden the sentiment that the heathen had no rights which a white man was bound to respect. If for the moment the English "bought" the land with coats and trinkets, before long they were to dispose by fraud of claims of the natives. In later years Roger Williams was to be shocked to see the saints dispense even with coats and trinkets and extort rich lands from the Indians in the guise of judicial punishments or through forcible persuasion by military expeditions.

The significance of Williams' attack on royal patents, in the long view of history, springs from its honorable position as the first American attack on the white man's imperialism. Modern critics of the dogma of the white man's burden would doubtless believe that Williams, although obscure in his statements, was on the right track. He insisted upon equitable treatment of the Indians in purchasing their lands and attacked the current practice of "Christian Kings" in blandly appropriating new countries by right of discovery. Williams, however, was speaking out of turn in an age when backward races were not understood to have any particular rights as independent nations. How far imperial arrogance was then carried may be seen in the charter which Charles I granted to Lord Baltimore, which contained a provision that no one should recognize claims of the Indians to any part of the lands assigned in the grant. International law of the seventeenth century, created by world powers and designed for their ends, sanctioned the practice which Williams protested.

During the nine months following the affair of the patent, Williams reputedly was involved in two minor controversies centering in Salem. One concerned scriptural warrant for the appearance of women in church without wearing veils; the other, the Puritan scruple against the cross in the English ensign as a popish superstition. Neither episode brought Williams into direct conflict with the authorities, but each furnished the later Puritan chroniclers, Hubbard and Cotton Mather, with rich materials for ridicule of Williams' tender conscience.

Holy Writ revealed that no woman should prophesy or pray with her head "uncovered." The question whether this enjoined veils had been agitated in England, and in March, 1634, it reappeared in Massachusetts. William Hubbard's anecdotes of the celebrated exile from Massachusetts included an account of Williams as the ludicrous champion of the wearing of veils. Williams had, indeed, the full measure of Puritan literalness and, as Hubbard alleged, may have drawn instances from the Bible to sanction the practice in Salem church. Other than this fallible tradition, recorded nearly five decades after the event, there is little to show that Williams figured largely in this curious and typical Puritan controversy. The real agitator in the affair was John Endecott, and the dispute began in Boston and not Salem. On March 7, 1634, during the regular Thursday lectures John Cotton spoke upon the question of veils and denied their necessity. The magistrate of Salem happened to be present and had his own ideas. Endecott spoke his mind, a wrangle followed, good fellowship seemed on the point of being forgotten, and the meeting reached the point of "some earnestness" when Governor Winthrop intervened and induced the fire-eaters to "brake-off." Sometime afterwards Cotton preached a sermon at Salem which immediately put an end to the wearing of veils. His most effective persuasion was the example of Tamar the Harlot whose reason for wearing a veil did not commend itself to Puritan maids and goodwives. It is an interesting sidelight on the little comedy that John Cotton himself, while still in the mother country, seems to have thought favorably of veiling the charms of the ladies when they were engaged in divine worship.

The controversy precipitated in November, 1634, when the cross was cut from the flag was more crucial and, with the help of the later great novelist of Salem, was to become celebrated. Nathaniel Hawthorne in the nineteenth century worked it into a dramatic story in which Endecott was the hero. William Hubbard in the seventeenth century worked it into a satirical attack in which Williams was the villain. Hubbard was official historian of the Bay and knew both Winthrop's account and the records of the colony. Neither Winthrop nor the colony records mention any responsibility of Williams. By contrast, Hubbard's account is illuminating:

> Another notion diffused by him occasioned more disturbance, for in his zeal for advancing the purity of reformation, and abolishing all badges of superstition, he inspired some persons of great interest in that place, that the cross in the King's colors ought to be taken away as a relic of antichristian superstition. What that good man would have done with the cross upon his coin, (if he had any left,) that bore that sign of superstition, is uncertain. But this notion about the King's colors prevailed with some so far, that it was taken out of the ensign at Salem by one in place. . . . In this manner did overheated zeal vent itself in the said Mr. Williams, of whom they were wont to say in Essex, where he lived, that he was divinely mad; as if his too much zeal, as Festus said of Paul's too much learning, had made him beside himself.

The "one in place" was Endecott, although neither Hubbard nor Cotton Mather, who repeats the story, felt it necessary at that point to mention his name. Since enemies in England might seize on it as "a kind of rebellion to deface the King's colors," the magistrates decided to bring the culprits to book. They levied no accusation against Williams. Richard Davenport who had carried the defaced colors received a summons; and at the general court on May 6, 1634, Endecott was deprived for a year of all public offices. The magistrates were not more severe on the Salem assistant because they were all "persuaded he did it out of tenderness of conscience."

Williams was one of those who disliked the red cross of St. George as a relic of popery, but as in the controversy over the veils his responsibility was secondary. Hubbard, in 1680, constrained to make the most of the "dangerous opinions" of the exile from Massachusetts, described Endecott as "bewitched" by Williams. John Endecott, however, was a man who generally could stand stoutly on his own legs and take responsibility for his own actions. He was a distinguished founder of the colony, long an assistant and for some years governor, and a man of wealth with a considerable investment in the Massachusetts Bay Company. It is understandable why Williams was saddled by Cotton, Hubbard, Morton, and others with "singular opinions" while little was said of the identical scruples of Endecott and the saints. The outcome of the controversy was to show still more clearly that not Roger Williams alone, nor Endecott, but magistrates, ministers, and a large part of the population were capable of singular opinions and "over-heated zeal." Throughout the year of 1635 the agitation against the cross in the flag steadily mounted, so that court and colony became divided; and although these were the months when Laud's attack on the Massachusetts charter roused grave fear, the magistrates finally gave leave for display of the ensign without the cross. Hooker wrote a treatise in defense of the cross, but Cotton threw his weight on the other side, being for this once of the same conscience as Roger Williams. For years to come the hated symbol was seen no more, and even at the end of the century Sewall and Mather "judged it a Sin" to have the cross put in again.

Williams' scruples sprang out of Puritanism. Governor Winthrop, on his visit to Plymouth in 1632, when passing a place named Hue's Cross, renamed it Hue's Folly lest the Papists take credit for it. Literalness, magnification of the trivial, absence of a sense of humor went with the age and with the doctrine of purity out of the Word. The notions of wearing veils and cutting out the cross were born of the selfsame logic that ensnared John Cotton in *Moses, His Judicialls.*

Although nothing Williams had done since his return from Plymouth had brought him into serious conflict with the ruling order, the trend of affairs must have filled him with misgivings. In the Bay colony by curious cross-breeding, the Holy Commonwealth beloved by the Puritans had sprung from the loins of an English company organized for trade. A government with plenary power over the life and liberty of English subjects was being fashioned from the patent of a business corporation. In conjunction with their Puritan lords spiritual, the transmigrated patentees of the company were making themselves holy stewards of a wilderness Zion, deriving, as they imagined, mediately from God a design for the winnowing of souls, the wooing of profits, and the elevation of the righteous to the seats of the mighty. The pattern of life and government in the Bay as it stood revealed in 1634 offered little peace of mind to men like Williams and boded ill for the high cause of a generous freedom. An English opposition had become a New England oligarchy. The patentees who came with the charter had made themselves omnipotent through the court of assistants, and in violation of their patent did not propose to share their supremacy. The landed interest and the clergy were in the saddle, and the process had already begun by which in forty-five years the ruling group manipulated the general court, successfully obtaining special grants of land for thirty-two of their circle for a munificent total of 57,214 acres, this in addition to large estates obtained through the channel of town allotments.

The bulwark of power lay in the suffrage, and in May, 1631, the court of assistants ordered that none should be freemen unless they were church members. This limitation on the suffrage was decisive and insured domination by the close alliance of ministers and magistrates; for "church members" were not the whole body of the congregation but only those who had received admission into the select inner circle of "Visible Saints." Puritan clergy of theocratic bent took care to admit only men zealous in orthodoxy and well affected to the dominant order; and before long, English Puritans were startled to hear that in the new Zion over the seas three-fourths of the people had been shut out from membership in the church.

Yet already a rising protest warned the magistrates of the need of circumspection. To attract settlers and win their subjection to rule by the saints, the colony was making grants of small farms through the agency of the towns. So was formed a growing body of property owners, men who as freeholders would have enjoyed wider liberties in the mother country they had left; and in the face of these, "very jealous of their liberties," the magistrates were compelled to make concessions more in conformity with the charter. The men of Watertown in 1632 expressed fear that the assistants would bring "themselves and posterity into bondage"; before the year was out the freemen of the colony wrested from the assistants their proper right to elect the governor and deputy-governor. In 1634 they demanded and obtained a look at the charter, the terms of which had been concealed from the public. The result was that the freemen won the right to elect their own members as deputies to sit in the general court. But the victory was inconclusive. The body of freemen were restricted in number and their deputies subservient. When Deputy Stoughton in 1634 dared protest the irregular arrogation by the assistants of a veto on decisions made by the deputies, he was deprived for three years of public office. Men like Williams were to find virtually no protection for themselves against arbitrary rule and rigorous orthodoxy.

With a suffrage linked to sanctification, and clerical influence over the people employed as a stout crutch to support magisterial statecraft, oligarchy served well the dual purpose of keeping democracy out and orthodoxy in. Believing in wealth and power in the hands of the few, and dressing up magistracy as a divine stewardship, the assistants sanctioned their conduct by Higher Law when charter or English precedent would have tied their hands, and parried the popular clamor for a code of "known laws." The Massachusetts squirearchy, entrenched in the ranks of assistants, clung to ultimate judicial authority, and the bulk of the legislative authority, and saw to it in the elections that these sinews of power did not change hands. Only the husks of political rights had been conceded to the rank and file of the "Saints"; the vast body of yeoman farmers and common folk remained unenfranchised, and any movement for redress faced insuperable odds.

It was inevitable that such overweening authority should meet with challenge, and that challenge when made might not be fruitless. Before the end of 1634 Roger

Williams ran afoul of the rising oligarchy in good earnest. In November he received a summons from the court on the grounds that he had again impugned charters by challenging the king's title to the lands of the Indians and had also termed the churches of England "antichristian." Five months later, on April 8, 1635, he was likewise accused of teaching that "a magistrate ought not to tender an oath to an unregenerate man." Events were taking a more serious turn. Williams was no longer merely one of those whom Winthrop castigated as "troublers of Israel." He was, from the magisterial view, on the road to rebellion.

THE SALEM REBELLION

The proceedings which led up to the banishment of Williams really began in November, 1634. Prior to that time nothing had occurred which foreshadowed his expulsion. It was true that some of the "offenses" which were later cited as grounds for banishment had made their appearance. Williams had already questioned the authority of magistrates to enforce penalties for breach of the first table, and he had been dealt with by the magistrates in connection with his treatise against the patent. These difficulties had been ironed out. It was the series of events from November, 1634, to October of the following year which made the final break inevitable.

At this fateful November meeting the general court brought up two counts against Williams. One was his unquenchable Separatism: he was preaching that the churches of England were false churches; the other and more serious was that Williams "had broken his promise to us, in teaching publickly against the king's patent, and our great sin in claiming right thereby to this country." The breach of promise alleged by Winthrop was probably not a breach of any formal oath, since at the time of his previous summons about the patent Williams simply gave "satisfaction of his intention and loyalty." Interpreting Williams' conciliatory spirit on that occasion as substantially a pledge of silence, the magistrates were the more irate because this was not a case of a mere manuscript shown to authorities in private. Williams was now "teaching publickly." Taking prompt action, the magistrates summoned him to the next court.

The reason why Williams had raised the issue of the patent in public can only be surmised. In 1647 Cotton charged that he "pressed upon the Magistrates and People" to repent in "dayes of solemne Humilitation" and return the patent to the king. Williams' version in answer to Cotton, was that he proposed an address to the king to secure modification "of that part of the Pattent which respects the Donation of Land." Otherwise the sin "could not be Expiated" except by returning to England again, leaving the land to its native owners and making public acknowledgment and confession of the "Evill." This latter suggestion was sheer idealistic fantasy, though of interest as showing that Williams was thinking strongly of human rights irrespective of race. The other alternative was obviously imprudent, for to invite the king to reconsider the patent would strengthen its enemies. To hold days of humiliation was more thinkable and well in accord with the Puritan practice of bewailing public sins to appease the wrath of a just God. Yet to clergy and magistrates there was no need for humiliation; New England was the promised land of God's chosen people.

At the meeting of March 3, 1635, the

court took no action either on Williams' Separatist indictment of English churches or his views on the patent, probably because of the intervention of John Cotton and the brethren who felt that Williams' "violent course" sprang from scruples of conscience rather than "seditious" intent. Cotton's account throws a shaft of light on the dual authority of church and state: "I presented (with the consent of my fellow-Elders and Brethren) a serious Request to the Magistrates, that they would be pleased to forbeare all civill prosecution against him, till our selves (with our Churches) had dealt with him in a Church way, to convince him of sinne." The governor, presumably Thomas Dudley, warned Cotton that the clergy were deceived in Roger Williams, if they thought that he would "condescend to learne of any of us," but in spite of this pessimism Cotton's request was approved and the brethren undertook to labor with the recalcitrant of Salem.

The device of dealing with offenders through consociation already had proved a formidable weapon of social pressure. A battery of confident and capable Puritan priests was generally an irresistible answer to a doubting Thomas; nor were such advice and admonition unavailing with Williams. Although there is no evidence that he yielded his Separatist position as to the churches of England, the brethren won him to silence on the score of the patent. On none of the three subsequent occasions when Williams appeared before the court was the charge renewed that he was agitating against the charter. "Councells from Flesh and Bloud suppresst" his intended letter to the king, Williams confessed later, although, as he shrewdly pointed out, this did not prevent the rulers of the colony from seizing the stratagem of "Worldly policy" and making his earlier activities against the patent a "cause" of banishment.

The tortuous uses which the assistants were making of the charter which they defended so carefully from the attack of Williams are not without pertinence. On April 1, 1634, these magistrates sat for the last time as the general court of the colony. Two months later the freemen discovered the flagrant violation of the charter by which the inner oligarchy had defrauded them of legislative power and in consequence rejected Winthrop for governor for a number of years. Meanwhile, on April 1, Winthrop, Dudley, Coddington, Endecott, Ludlow, Bradstreet, Nowell, and Pynchon voted themselves and their group special colonial grants of lands apart from their allotments from the towns where they lived. Among the *douceurs* voted privileged dignitaries, 200 acres of choice land went to John Wilson, minister of Boston; 200 to Assistant Nowell; 500 to Dudley, Deputy-Governor; and to the wealthy newcomer, John Haynes, Esq., soon to be governor, a full thousand acres. In preceding years they had already granted Winthrop 650 acres; Dudley 200, bringing his new total to 700 acres; Endecott 300, and smaller allotments to the assistants Bradstreet and Ludlow.

At this same meeting of April 1, 1634, the ruling clique in the colony adopted a measure which eventually induced Williams to take the road of opposition. The magistrates entrenched themselves behind a new requirement compelling inhabitants who were not freemen to take a "resident's oath" in which they swore to submit to the laws and authority of the governor and magistrates and to "give speedy notice" of any sedition "plotted or intended against the . . . government. Soe helpe mee God." The occasion of the oath, John Cotton affirmed, was "Intelligence of some Episcopall, and malignant practices against the Countrey" on the part of their enemies in England. But John Cotton did not explain the full significance of the oath. "Let men only look over to the fruits of their principles in New England," wrote Robert Baillie of Scotland, who had heard Roger Williams' version. To Baillie, the Massachusetts oath smacked of disloyalty to England. Upon "suspition," he said, that the king might have their patent altered, "they did quickly purchase and distribute Armes among all their people, and exact of every one an Oath for the defence of their Patent against all impugners whosoever." John Cotton in 1647 passed lightly over the damaging fact that the magistrates secretly determined to resist recall of the charter and stooped to the gentle prevarication that the court was not "imposing" the oath but merely "offering" it. According to the actual records, the oath was to be tendered twice; residents who refused it a second time were to be banished

This dire penalty did not deter Roger Williams. The ideas that had already led him to impugn the patent virtually obligated him on the same grounds to attack the oath. "This Oath when it came abroad," wrote Cotton, "he vehemently withstood it, and disswaded sundry from it. . . ." As a non-freeman, Williams would be required to take the new oath and by its terms he would be forced to give a pledge to be "obedient and conformeable" and "submitt" to the "lawes and constitucions" of the colony. In substance, if the future democrat of Rhode Island had sworn to this, he would have taken oath to uphold the patent and to submit without opposition to the dictates of the oligarchy.

Williams objected to the oath because it mixed the things of Caesar with the things that belonged to God. A magistrate made a mockery of religion if he tendered an oath to an unregenerate person. This was taking the name of God in vain—making an irreligious person swear and call God to witness. An oath was "a part of God's worship, and God's worship was not to be put upon carnall persons." Nor was it proper to employ an oath to cast a halo of sanctification over the officers and fiat of the civil authority. Williams harked back to his assertion of 1630 that enforcement of the first table was not the business of civil magistrates. As his ideas clarified, he felt it an abomination to invoke the name of God in swearing allegiance to a mere government of men. Later Williams was to state bluntly his belief that the magistrates and clergy of Massachusetts utilized the combined agency of church and state to bolster their privileged position. How far his thoughts had progressed by April, 1635, when he was summoned for opposing the oath, is a matter of surmise. We can at least be certain of his suspicion that the rulers of the Bay were employing an act of worship for political ends. As Cotton noted, Williams affirmed that an oath or covenant was "Christs Prerogative" alone. "So by his Tenent," lamented Cotton, neither Visible Saints nor other godly men might take the oath, "because it was the establishment not of Christ, but of mortall men in their office." This to Roger Williams smacked too strongly of oligarchy by divine right.

Williams' attack on the oath appeared to the founders of the Bay more obstreperous and menacing than any of his earlier actions and, as Baillie surmised, loomed large in his final trial. "Mr. Williams opposition to this Oath, as he alledgeth, was the cheife cause of his banishment." Summoned before the court on April 30, "he was heard," wrote Winthrop, "before all the ministers, and very clearly confuted." Endecott likewise opposed the oath, but presently "gave place to the truth." Confuting Williams consisted of a one-way debate in which the authorities simply expounded their side of the case and then voted that they had won. This process convinced neither Williams nor the people at large, and in the following months so many inhabitants joined Williams in refusing to take the oath that "the Court was forced to desist from that proceeding." On this issue Williams had won.

On July 8, 1635, the young Salem cleric was again hailed to court, charged with contending that magistrates had no power to punish breaches of the first table except in cases disturbing "the civil peace." This return to his old Separatist heresy grew out of a recent action of the magistrates. On March 4 they called for a "uniforme" church discipline and clarification of the civil power to make it compulsory. Since this conception of church and state struck fundamentally at any idea of independent congregationalism, Williams openly challenged it. Summoned to account for this bold opposition, Williams was also charged with continued opposition to the oath and with certain annoying scruples that one ought not to pray with an unregenerate person or give thanks after sacraments or after meals.

Williams' opposition to civil enforcement of religious commandments struck at the vital spot in the armour of magistrates and clergy. When he faced his accusers on July 8, he discovered that leading ministers were there by special request. Their faces were hostile. Cotton and the brethren who had been laboring with Williams had finally determined to write Salem church to "admonish" him, and when, in the course of the lengthy proceeding, the magistrates called for advice, the clergy replied that by Williams' principles "a church might run into heresy, apostacy, or tyranny, and yet the civil magistrate could not intermeddle." Seeing clearly that the great recalcitrant of Salem had come close to stretching the old Separatist doctrine of Robert Browne into religious liberty, they told the court that such a man should "be removed."

Another matter highly prejudicial to Williams' case was a recent action of the Salem congregation in calling Williams as minister in place of Skelton, who had died the year before. This warm approval of one who was "under question" evoked the phantom of a free pulpit and a democratic congregationalism. Consulting together, the vigilant clerics and magistrates unanimously condemned Williams' opinions as "erroneous, and very dangerous" and censured Salem's action in making him minister as "a great contempt of authority." The magistrates granted "time" to Williams and his church "to consider of these things," but at the next general court Salem's minister must give satisfaction or else "expect the sentence."

As Williams heard these words, his thoughts may have flitted back to his earlier fears of a national church under strict "superintendency." The brethren had replied all too readily that "no church or person" could have power over another church. The falsity of those assurances now stood naked.

Before Williams left the court that day he was to see any pretense of a free church abandoned. Unwittingly the town of Salem played into the hands of the magistrates and clergy by petitioning for land in Marblehead Neck to which it had claim. The magistrates were delighted; here was an opportunity for a brilliant stratagem to force Salem church to reconsider its contempt. They rejected the petition "because they had chosen Mr. Williams" while he stood under question. The Salem representatives endeavored to submit proof of the town's title to the land which, Salem alleged later, "would have given satisfaction might they have had leave to speak. . . ." The frankness of the court was admirable. No trial of legal right of the town to the land would be permitted. It was a warning that the oligarchy held all the cards.

The sentiments of Williams and Endecott and the congregation, following this threat of sentence upon Salem's minister and the peremptory dismissal of the town petition, may well be imagined. Salem church held an indignation meeting at which Williams and his followers drove further in the direction of democratic congregationalism. The ministers and magistrates who had intended the other churches to advise Salem church to admonish Roger Williams found the tables turned. Salem wrote to the other churches "to admonish the magistrates" for their "heinous sin, and likewise the deputies."

In the Massachusetts of 1635 this was an extraordinary procedure. Williams and Salem, resorting to something of a modern democratic device, were appealing over the heads of the politicians to their constituents. Since only Visible Saints or church members were freemen, they alone could normally bring pressure on the general court. The letters from Salem, criticising not simply the inner oligarchy of the assistants but the deputies as well, constituted an appeal not only to the small body of the enfranchised but to the whole people in their separate congregations.

The magistrates and clergy dared not risk a backfire from their constituents and were prompt to scotch such a democratic precedent. Through their connivance, the elders quietly pocketed the letters and they never were read to the people in the congregations. Oligarchy must rule in church as well as state and the common man in the congregation must not be heard.

Salem church was incensed. The authorities not only challenged its clear right to choose its teacher but now assailed its right to communicate with other churches. The congregation met for a heated discussion and Williams and the lay elder, Samuel Sharpe, drafted a letter of protest to the elders at Boston. Boston magistrates, reading this letter, could no longer doubt Williams' heresy as to civil authority: to punish Salem church by refusing land to the town was "to deal with a church out of a church way." Nor could Cotton and Wilson mistake Williams' radical demand for a democratic church: "We have not yet apprehended it to be the choice of the officers of a church, when public letters are sent from sister Churches, to deliver or not to deliver the letters unto the body. . . ." Affairs of the congregation belonged "to the whole body" rather "than to one or all the elders." Salem did not hold with the belief that "the people are weak . . . giddy and rash, and therefore should not enjoy such liberties."

This plea for free government and a free church fell on deaf ears. During August and September the magistrates and clergy joined forces to wean Salem from Williams, hoping thereby to maneuver him into a position where they could deal with him without embarrassment. Hooker, Cotton, and the elders brought pressure on the saints of Salem to repudiate the "offensive" opinions and practices of their pastor. Their labors were aided by a fortuitous event which they triumphantly hailed as a judgment of God. Because Williams continued to dispute the holy testimony of the brethren, "it pleased the Lord," said Cotton, "to stop his mouth, by a sodaine disease." While stricken "neare unto death," Williams engaged in painful self-searching and found no cause for remorse. Magistrates and clergy, he now knew, would relent only upon his retraction and submission. His only rightful course as a Separatist was to strike for the independence of his church. A majority of his congregation had already joined him in professing the necessity of separating from the false churches of England. It was now equally necessary to "come out" from the churches of the Bay. Williams rallied himself on his sickbed and composed a letter to his congregation. The Massachusetts churches, he contended, had stumbled from the way, and Salem must free itself of such spiritual jurisdiction. For his own part, he could not walk betwixt Christ and Antichrist. To submit without faith was sin; he could not continue as pastor unless the church purged itself by a separation.

Meanwhile a committee of ministers drew up a "Model of Church and Civil Power" which they sent to Salem. It was a sober warning that if a church grew schismatical or corrupt, the civil magistrates could strike down those who corrupted it. Toleration of other religions, it said, would dissolve the state as well as the church. The civil authorities could therefore compel church attendance, coerce an offensive church, and forbid any independent churches.

Not without reason did the little oligarchy speak of its members as "Gods upon earth"; nor did the magistrates shrink from the course of narrow repression which the committee of ministers outlined. On September 3, to put an end once for all to the opposition in Salem, the oligarchy struck and struck hard. The general court unseated the deputies of the town and sent them home; the freemen, or Visible Saints of Salem, were to have no representation until they disclaimed the church letters, nor would the court hear their claim to land in the Neck until the church repented of its choice of Williams. This stern action showed clearly enough how far the oligarchy would go in coercing a church and in beating down any public criticism of magisterial policy. Dismayed, yet furious, John Endecott appeared defiantly before the authorities and attempted to justify the Salem letters. This was *lèse-majesté*. Peremptorily refusing him a hearing, the court ordered Endecott imprisoned for contempt. There had been no more vigorous and independent figure in the ruling class of the Bay than John Endecott, but it was now shown him that he would reap little if he opposed his fellow-dignitaries. In a little while his head cooled, and "he came and acknowledged his fault, and was discharged."

The tide had begun to turn. Salem had moved surprisingly far, and a part of the congregation were ready to follow their pastor into absolute separation, even if it meant exile; but if the majority had to make choice between Roger Williams and the Puritan oligarchy, the choice was not to be Williams. The greater part of the church, declared Williams, "was swayed and bowed (whether for feare of persecution or otherwise) to say and practise what, to my knowledge, . . . many of them mourned under." The oligarchy had more to offer in the way of tangible persuasions, and slowly during the month of September, Williams witnessed the town inclining toward submission. It remained only for the magistrates to deal with the great leader of the remonstrants. The back of the Salem rebellion was broken.

OLIGARCHY IN THE JUDGMENT SEAT

Although the magistrates warned Williams on July 8 to give satisfaction at the next court or "to expect the sentence," they shrewdly held their hand until they had pressed Salem down into the ruts of orthodoxy. By the time of his trial Williams was isolated, his cause lost, and the sentence of the court a foregone conclusion. On his way to the trial Cotton told a friend that the magistrates were so "incensed" that the verdict was certain.

The general court of October 8, 1635, was not an ordinary assemblage. Because of the importance of Williams' case, all the ministers of the Bay had been requested to attend. Cotton and other worthies who believed in severity against those who questioned the ways of the oligarchy had the support of the wealthy John Haynes, now governor, and of two new arrivals, the energetic Hugh Peter who was soon to succeed Williams as minister of Salem, and narrow-minded John Wilson, just back from England. Williams soon had clear indication of the judgment he could expect from men of such stamp. The court found John Smith of Dorchester guilty of broaching "dyvers dangerous opinions" and sentenced him to banishment.

Later in the day came the celebrated trial of Salem's pastor. Williams' heresy in denying the coercive power of the state in matters of religion and the other charges of July 8 were again presented. The court added new charges concerning the offensive Salem letters and Williams' plea to Salem church to separate from the churches of the Bay. Given leave to speak, Salem's fiery Separatist stood up stoutly, justified the letters, and "maintained all his opinions."

Magistrates like Winthrop knew Williams' sterling qualities of mind and heart and they valued them too well not to offer him one final chance. After hesitation the court granted him a month's respite. But the accused man knew he was offered no final escape; for he could save himself only by retraction and submission. Since there was no point in delay, he requested "to dispute presently."

Hooker, of whom it was said that so great was his majesty he could put a king in his pocket, was selected to confute the heretic. During the disputation Williams complained "he was wronged by a slanderous report up and downe the Countrey, as if he did hold it to be unlawful for a Father to call upon his childe to eate his meate." Hooker, a skilled dialectician, thereupon set a trap for his young opponent. "Why, saith he, you will say as much againe, (if you stand to your own Principles) or be forced to say nothing." Williams was "confident he should never say it." Hooker then seized on Williams' contention that it was unlawful to call on an unregenerate person to take an oath or pray. If a child was unregenerate, he could not properly pray God to bless his meat. But according to the Bible it was improper to eat meat unsanctified by prayer. Thus, concluded Hooker, "it is unlawful for you to call upon him to eate it." This confutation, according to Cotton, forced Williams into silence. Winthrop, however, recorded after the trial that not even Hooker could reduce him from his errors.

The modern mind is not so impressed

by ingenious dialectics as Hooker and Cotton. What Hooker demonstrated was the intellectual confusion which could flow from the Puritan effort to join systematic logic with scriptural literalness. Wedded to the dogma of Non-separatism, Cotton and his associates could see in Williams' obduracy merely proof that he was "sinning against the light of his own Conscience." If a man stood to his principles after the elders reasoned with him, then that was not his conscience but his obstinacy. Williams, on the other hand, was groping toward a more scientific understanding of the mind of mankind. As an authentic Separatist, he was not committed to the dogma that all must agree, none should oppose, and any who criticized the lords temporal or lords spiritual must be silenced or banished. It was a courageous man who could be a good man and still differ with his fellows. But Williams was not chained by the rigid compulsions which dominated the Puritan minds that passed judgment upon him. He did not believe that his opinions must be wrong because authority said so. Unlike John Cotton in 1637, he could not argue himself into a sense of error merely because the magistrates demanded it.

As the formality of "confuting" Williams proceeded, the sun slowly sank over the horizon. Williams knew that his voice was lost in that place of gathering darkness. The magistrates were now ready to give sentence; "yet night being come, the Court arose and enjoyned him to appeare the next morning." Williams still had a night to sleep on it, a respite granted presumably in the hope that he might lose his nerve. It was not a peaceful night for the great recalcitrant of Salem, but no still small voice whispered to him that he was wrong.

Unshaken and unflinching, he appeared before the court in the morning to receive sentence. Governor Haynes, who within a few months was to criticize Winthrop for too great leniency, stood up and summarized the formal charges. Then, to identify the will of the court with the will of God, the governor pronounced the words of St. Paul: "Mark them which cause divisions and offences, contrary to the doctrine which ye have learned, and avoid them." The way to avoid such, as Haynes interpreted it, was "by banishment."

With this divine sanction—favorite of persecutors—ringing in his ears, Roger Williams heard the oligarchy pronounce the famous sentence to exile:

> Whereas Mr. Roger Williams . . . hath broached and divulged dyvers newe and dangerous opinions, against the aucthoritie of magistrates, as also writt letters of defamac̃on, both of the magistrates and churches here, and that before any convicc̃on, and yet mainetaineth the same without retracc̃on, it is therefore ordered, that the said Mr. Williams shall departe out of this jurisdicc̃on. . . .

There have been so many contradictory statements about the banishment that it seems worth while to review the chief points at issue. No other incident in Williams' life has aroused more protracted controversy. Almost from the date of the trial, the banishment became a *cause célèbre*. In the eyes of the law the issue may now be considered officially settled by the slightly ridiculous gesture of the Massachusetts general court in repealing the act of banishment in the year of Rhode Island's tercentenary. Yet in most discussions of the banishment certain elements have been overlooked; and moreover the banishment itself still has meaning in its reflec-

rofound and recurrent conflicts the impulse toward freedom orces of repression.

The chief controversy has centered upon the disagreement as to the principal causes of Williams' banishment, the motives of the magistrates and ministers, and the necessity or justice of their decision. Since there has been little disposition to contest the legality of the banishment, the issue has been largely whether Williams was sentenced for political reasons or for religious beliefs. The classical view in Rhode Island has been that Williams espoused the cause of religious liberty in Massachusetts and that the persecuting Puritans banished him because of it. The opposing view has made the attack on the charter the chief cause of banishment and has presented Williams' trial as a case of sedition.

Cotton and Williams had their first exchange on the subject soon after the latter's flight to Rhode Island. It was but natural for that sharp-tongued son of Rhode Island, Samuel Gorton, to assert bluntly that Williams was banished "for dissenting in some points about church government"; and for John Clarke, himself expelled as an Antinomian, to cry persecution and to publicize the case of Williams as another expulsion "for matter of conscience." Within a decade the banishment became celebrated on both sides of the Atlantic as one of many instances of severity charged against Massachusetts. New England Puritans, who had long groaned under persecution in England and who had cried out against it as persecution of God's people, smarted under the accusation that they had become persecutors in turn. Disconcerted and indignant, they undertook to place the onus on Williams, on the Antinomians, on the Baptists, the Quakers, and the long train of persons, men and women, who suffered the lash, the halter, or the sentence of banishment at the hands of the godly in New England. "Persecutours," remarked Williams drily, "endure not so to be called."

In this long, acrimonious debate, Massachusetts Puritans strove to rebut the accusation that they had become Separatists. To this they gave the pat answer that Separatists or schismatics were banished from the state—for political reasons—and excommunicated from the church for sinning against conscience. In 1641 Cotton hit upon this interesting distinction in giving alarmed conservatives in England fervent assurance that New England had not sunk into Separatism: "I answer, God forbid, God forbid: It is true, one Sheba of Bickry blew a Trumpet of such a seditious Separation; I meane one Mr. Williams late Teacher of Salem"; but he and others of that ilk "were all excommunicated out of the Church and banished out of the Common-wealth." "See therefore," cried Cotton, "how unjustly we are slandered for renouncing communion with you."

Cotton's *Letter to Mr. Williams,* appearing in London bookstalls in 1643, presented the expulsion of Williams as a "civill banishment." This was an invidious distinction, but it served the double purpose of disclaiming Separatism and at the same time disclaiming persecution. Edward Winslow of Plymouth colony similarly tried to clear Massachusetts of the charge of intolerance. In 1646 when representing the interests of the two colonies in London, he turned hotly on Gorton's reference to the persecution of Williams and declared "God cals mee at this time to take off these aspersions." He then followed Cotton's cue and by concentrating on the political causes of

Williams' banishment contrived to make Williams' expulsion a case of civil banishment.

A year later, in his *Reply to Mr. Williams,* John Cotton made an elaborate disquisition on the same theme. He gave the flat lie to Williams, charging that his statement of the causes of banishment was "fraudulent." Williams' contention that the civil power extended "onely to the bodies, and goods, and outward state of men" and his Separatist objection to hearing ministers in English parishes, Cotton dismissed as "no causes at all." The real causes were Williams' "seditious opposition against the Patent, and against the Oath of fidelitie." There were also two secondary factors: Williams' letters admonishing the magistrates; and his Separatism and "spreading of his Leaven to sundry that resorted to him." These last two counts, although incidental, "hastened" the sentence. The argument followed that the trial represented "prosecution," not persecution. Roger Williams was not banished at all but simply deported—for civil offenses. "I did never belieeve," affirmed Cotton, "that the sentence passed against him was an act of Persecution." "Master Cotton," retorted Williams, "knows not his own desire."

The pages of Winthrop's *Journal* furnish a sufficient refutation of Cotton's charge that Williams had given a fraudulent explanation of his trial, and one may conclude that Williams, Clarke, and Gorton had good reason to consider that the banishment was not simply political. Precisely because church and state were so nicely dovetailed, the political and religious became nearly indistinguishable. "The frame or constitution" of the Bay churches, as Williams retorted to Cotton, was "implicitly National." "Otherwise," demanded Williams, "why was I not yet permitted to live in the world, or Common-weale, except for this reason, that the Common weale and Church is yet but one, and hee that is banished from the one, must necessarily bee banished from the other also." By contrast, "particular Churches,"—Separatists and other liberal sects which did not believe in a state church—expelled unworthy persons merely "from their particular societies," and heretics "may still live in the Countrey . . . unmolested by them."

Contemporaries found the attempt to shift responsibility to Williams and absolve Massachusetts of persecution anything but convincing. Heresy and sedition in Massachusetts were inextricably joined, and only by artful casuistry could Cotton contrive to deny it. A little less than a decade after the banishment of Williams, the English divine, Thomas Edwards, thrust home through the Massachusetts defense: "They found out a pretty fine distinction to deceive themselves with, that the magistrate questioned and punished for those opinions and errors not as heresies and such opinions, but as breaches of the civil peace and disturbance to the Common-wealth."

Although it is sometimes contended that Williams' views on the first table were of little or no consequence among the causes of banishment, Winthrop's account, the public admonition to Salem written by Cotton and the Boston elders, and Governor Haynes' summary at the trial, all show that such a supposition is clearly wrong. It is also questioned whether the heresies for which Williams was tried included a belief in religious liberty; his proposition about the first table, it is asserted, never meant such a large principle. In his later tracts Williams harked back to the question of the first table, saying repeatedly that magistrates could not punish religious offenses without exceeding their lawful authority. Though this position was necessarily pivotal in his whole later conception of the separate spheres of church and state, it is urged that Williams did not understand the point so clearly in 1635; there was a difference between the original intention and the final result.

To take this view is to strain at a gnat and swallow a camel. Obviously at the time of trial Williams demanded no less than toleration of dissent. The assembled ministers at the court on July 8 made no mistake when they pointed out in consternation that Williams' proposal would be fatal to their object of compulsory uniformity. By such a principle, as Cotton wrote Salem in 1635, the churches could do no more than admonish a wayward congregation; though a church dissented so abominably as to fall into "papism," the civil magistrate could not compel it.

At the time of his trial Williams was taking the usual position of the extreme Separatists who attacked the whole system of national churches. Thence came his efforts at Salem to carry democratic congregationalism to its logical conclusion. More truly than Robert Browne before him, he was seeking a reformation without tarrying for any. An authentic Separatist, he attacked the consociation of ministers as leading to a national church system, insisted on the autonomy of local congregations, and, when the government interfered at Salem, held Separatist meetings in his own house. These actions, coupled with his views on the first table, mark him already in 1635 a believer in radical Independency, an avowed advocate of free churches in a free state.

Williams' belief as to the first table, as Cotton, Hooker, and Hugh Peter knew, was a cardinal doctrine of Separatists, Baptists, and the independent sects. Logical on its own premises, contending that truth could defend itself without the use of force, that regeneration was inward and individual and outward compulsion powerless to promote spirituality, Separatism could never be palatable to authoritarian Puritans. Nonseparatists in New England well knew its consequences. Enraptured by the vision of the disciplined uniformity of the great church militant, they shrank from the schisms and brawls which divided the ranks of English Independents in the mother country and Holland. Cherishing the eternal hope of rising to power in the English church, orthodox saints could do no other than condemn Williams' denial of use of the civil sword to compel uniformity. Had the magistrates done otherwise, Massachusetts would have entered on the high road to toleration.

To contend that Williams' demand for the right to dissent played little part in his trial and sentence is to take the hazardous view that the ministers and magistrates were strangely unmindful of their dearest convictions. In 1635 Roger Williams had grasped the central point of his later famed theory of religious liberty as a natural right. Hubbard was not wide of the mark when he listed as a cause of banishment a demand for liberty of conscience and an "unlimited toleration of all religions."

Although Williams spoke for the future, for the liberation of man, he has long had reputation as one who brought his sentence upon his own head. In the eyes of the magistrates and their later defenders, he was "a dangerous intruder and an agent of mischief." He was accused of having an unsettled judgment and pride of opinion. He "had a zeal," declared Hubbard, and added subsequently, "too much zeal." That celebrated nineteenth century Puritan, John Quincy Adams, adjudged him guilty of "conscientious contentiousness." John Palfrey diagnosed his case as *certaminas gaudia,* the joy of quarrel. But a contemporary of Palfrey and Adams, that ardent Jacksonian Democrat, George Bancroft, had a different understanding: "If he was charged with pride, it was only for the novelty of his opinions."

Williams' scruples of conscience sometimes did and sometimes did not coincide with those of the rulers of the Bay, but his contentiousness and supposed self-pride were scarcely proper grounds for expulsion from the colony. There had been nothing scandalous in his conduct. He had committed no offense of the sort which he afterwards defined so accurately as violations of the civil peace; he had not offended against the "life, chastity, goods or good name" of any one in the colony. He was "a man lovely in his carriage," declared Winslow. Stewards of the Lord might tell themselves that opposition to their will could only spring from pride and self-conceit; yet magistrates and clergy alike admitted Williams' integrity and sincerity, the high order of his intellectual attainments, and the warm humanity of his character. If the banishment were to be defended, it should be on grounds other than the personal characteristics of Roger Williams.

The most frequent defense of the banishment has centered on the attack on the patent. Williams had all the effrontery of a belligerent democrat. By questioning the charter, he attacked the power of the king; by assailing the cross in the flag, he attacked the king's abuse of true religion; by advocating the rigid Separation, he attacked the royalist church. These agitations, coming precisely at the time when the royal government was actively hostile, would seem highly embarrassing to the men who had established a government of saints in the Wilderness Zion. Presented from this single point of view, the banishment becomes a justifiable action of self-defense.

This view, that Williams' criticism of the charter jeopardized the rights and liberty of the people of Massachusetts, leads to certain difficulties. As the simple facts of chronology show, John Cotton, who pounced on the affair of the charter as an easy rebuttal of the charge of persecution, strained the evidence. The last occasion on which Williams is known to have preached against the patent was in 1634. There is no record of new outbursts after the meeting of the court on November 27, when Williams was summoned. Williams still believed that the patent should be modified but he "supprest" his objections. Ten months later at the trial, the oligarchy seized the opportunity to rake up this older charge, but if it entered into the judgment of the court, it was more as an added irritant and convenient excuse than as an immediate menace to Massachusetts' security.

From these facts of chronology it would appear that Cotton was guilty of distortion, and that the issue of the charter was scarcely preëminent at the time of the trial. No evidence has been found that Williams' conduct in Massachusetts in any way increased the royal animosity against Massachusetts or that Charles and Laud ever knew of his attack on the charter. Williams' "sedition" in the matter never reached the point of constituting a direct immediate threat to the state, whether one regards the imperial government at home as the state or whether one takes the highly irregular position of the Massachusetts oligarchy and views the colony as more or less an independent state.

Williams neither provoked the proceedings against the Massachusetts charter nor influenced their course. The responsibility for the writ of *quo warranto* must be placed squarely where it belongs, upon the rival colonial ambitions of the Massachusetts company and Gorges and Mason, and upon the conflict between the holy purposes of the Bay oligarchy and the no less holy purposes of Laud. In this conflict, the magistrates, by ignoring the call for the charter, were obstructing the course of English justice in proceedings which were undoubtedly legal; and, by preparing for armed resistance, they were involved in a far more flagrant defiance of lawful authority than any they could charge to Roger Williams. The actual danger of success in the *quo warranto* proceedings and of effective royal intervention is now known to have been remote. That danger, such as it was, would not have diminished if the young agitator of Salem had been ejected ten months sooner; nor, had the charter been vacated, would historians attribute its loss to Roger Williams.

The question of the charter has been often confused by the supposition that that document was the cornerstone of Massachusetts liberties. It was rather the cornerstone of power for the small and arbitrary group which sat in judgment on Williams. It was the bulwark behind which for more than a generation this group repressed the upthrust of the submerged population and established a system of ironclad rule. These men who resented Williams' scruples about the charter had embarked upon a course of flagrant and oppressive violations of that same charter. It is not apparent, therefore, that any concern of the magistrates and clergy for the charter was actuated by the desire to defend Massachusetts liberties and the cause of free government.

There is strong evidence that it was not Williams' disrespectful remarks about royal authority but the disrespect which he showed for their own authority which infuriated the leaders of the Bay. This is indicated in the very phraseology of the sentence of banishment. That sentence contains no mention of seditious attack upon royal authority but charges Roger Williams with dangerous opinions "against the aucthoritie of magistrates." The founders of Massachusetts, already thinking of themselves as rulers of a state virtually independent, were quick to resent attacks on magisterial power; and for the same reason, were prepared to flout even the prerogative of royal Charles, which was the real aspect of sedition in the eyes of English law. This determination to rule in their own house, to suppress any possible threat to their own supremacy, dictated alike their resistance to the royal government and their severity toward dissidents in the Bible commonwealth.

For a larger understanding of Williams' banishment, one must turn to his attack on the oath of submission in 1635 and to the Salem rebellion, in which he appealed to public opinion and led an opposition to the governing class. He never placed in jeopardy the provisions for self-government in the Massachusetts charter. The crime of Roger Williams was that he dared to oppose and to appeal to the people. If his agitations never struck at the right of home rule, they raised the forbidden question of who should rule at home.

Political and ecclesiastical expediency and the principle of religious intolerance dictated the expulsion. Chief responsibility for the banishment may be charged to two elements in the ethos of the Bay colony: the dogmatic requirements of the ecclesiastical establishment and the aristocratic requirements of magisterial domination. The magistrates and their clerical auxiliaries had combined to establish an authoritarian church and a government by oligarchy. Nor could the philosophy of men who made religious worship the monopoly of one church and political power the monopoly of a class allow them to consider that any could question that their sentence was just. In the very year of Williams' banishment, the clergy reported that it was not the will of the lawgiver but the divine purpose behind the law which made it binding. "Judges are Gods upon earthe," maintained the magistrates. The Stuarts contended for divine right in England with never more confidence than the new pretenders in the colony of saints. Nor did the clergy of the Bay, preaching the famous Biblical injunction to be submissive, allow their flocks to conceive otherwise: ". . . the powers that be are ordained of God. Whosoever therefore resisteth the power, resisteth the ordinance of God: and they that resist shall receive to themselves damnation. . . . Wherefore *Ye* must needs be subject, not only for wrath, but also for conscience sake." Intoxicated by this doctrine, John Cotton intimated to Williams that God himself had moved the court to pronounce the sentence.

Formal charges in a case like Williams' seldom cover all considerations. The religious thinking of the magistrates of the Bay was not the single deterministic element in their social and political philosophy. No one can deny the factor of religious aspiration, but concentration of power, whether in Massachusetts of the Puritan epoch or in other communities and other times, had a upon class ambition and vantage. Middle-class En had struggled against thei control taxation, destroy the monopolies of royal favorites, and sway national policy to favor their interests, lost none of their zest for power and wealth in the act of passage over the Atlantic. If the builders of the Bay colony were Puritans as well as Englishmen, their sense of a sacred calling shook none of their faith in the concept of class which flourished in the homeland. Their aristocratic view of the many as vicious and the few as the wise made it logical to assume that the elect should rule and the unregenerate submit. If they translated this into practice through an exclusive church membership linked to the suffrage, making qualified voters of Visible Saints, such joining of the politically privileged with the spiritually elect was but a Puritan rephrasing of the ancient identification of the wealthy and powerful with the wise and the good.

The close control which the oligarchy maintained upon public office, political franchise, and upon press, pulpit, and election sermons, was not simply relevant to religious zeal. Zealous magistrates and dignified clericals were not insensible of the perquisites of power, and the first families in Massachusetts like those in other colonies obtained advantages for themselves in land and income. In 1634 the inhabitants of Boston feared that "the richer men would give the poorer sort no great proportions of land" and tried to elect town officers from the ranks of the plain people. Winthrop already had preempted eighteen hundred acres, Dudley seventeen hundred, and Saltonstall sixteen hundred. The common people obtained small allotments, but the larger landed interests utilized the town land system to reward the saints, converting it gradually from a communal enterprise to a system of local land companies exclusive in membership and keen for speculation.

Discriminations which worked to the disadvantage of the common people dotted the records of the general court. Lest labor profit by its scarcity and bargain with employers, the court followed the venerable practice of English squires and kept down wages by fixing the rates through the fiat of the lawmaker. Men and women of humble station were restrained by law from aping the gentry in matters of dress. Laws which provided for ignominious punishments allowed lesser penalties if the culprit was a gentleman. The concept of class, flavored with Puritanism, tinctured economic policy and permeated the statute book.

Neither awe of the magistrates nor injunctions of the clergy could prevent the people from resenting such discriminations. "The great questions that have troubled the country," admitted Winthrop in 1645, "are about the authority of the magistrates and the liberty of the people." Even upon the clergy fell the suspicion of overmuch worldliness and love of power. With the Bay clergy in mind as well as the English hierarchy, Roger Williams later attacked "hireling ministries" for love of "maintenance" and concern for self. John Cotton he suspected of "swimming with the streame of outward credit, and profit." The more downright and class-conscious Samuel Gorton openly castigated the Massachusetts clergy for cruelty, arrogance, and worldly ambition.

Protests like that of Williams were generally fruitless, and occasional concessions of political privileges were limited in the main to the small class of freemen upon whose support the oligarchy depended. Criticism from individuals or petitions from groups outside the court brought quick retaliation. So Eliot discovered in 1634; and Endecott and the people of Salem in 1635; and so also Vane, Coddington, and even John Cotton in 1637. When Robert Child and his fellow-remonstrants rose to ask—in language milder than that used in the parliaments of James and Charles—for guarantees of their rights as Englishmen, they were not only silenced but heavily fined. When Winthrop made his "little speech" in 1645, he told those who complained of the "yoke" of authority, that if they would not "endure" but would "murmur, and oppose," they desired not liberty but only a corrupt license. By narrowing its definition, he emptied liberty of its essential content. "Sedition," he declared, "doth properly signifie a going aside to make a party." The founders of New England conceived of liberty as the duty to submit. There was no right to oppose.

Only in this larger background can the suppression of the congregational movement in Salem and the banishment of its leader be seen in perspective. Roger Williams made no immediate frontal attack on the class structure by which magistrates and clergy perpetuated their power; the full development of his democratic ideas was only to come later. But here was a man already too suspiciously democratic, too resolutely a believer in the value of untrammelled public discussion; a man who agitated against the oath of submission and whose powers of persuasion won wide popular support; a schismatic who cared nothing for the dogma of one authoritarian church; an inspired apostle of the left-wing sects who denied that magistrates could pluck forth men whose consciences turned them from the path of orthodoxy. For such a man, the ministers and magistrates, revolving in the narrow orbit of conservative Puritanism and mundane ambitions, could find no place in the commonwealth they had compounded from the charter of a trading company and the written word of God and William Ames.

In evaluating the importance of particular offenses of Williams one deals with imponderables. The crucial matter was not the affair of the charter in 1634 but the agitations of 1635 turning on the oath, the first table, Separatism, democratic congregationalism, and the Salem letters. The Salem rebellion was in substance a demand for the right of setting up a democratic opposition to those who had obtained power. Williams demonstrated, to the scandal of clergy and magistrates, the possibilities of use of the pulpit to awaken a popular resistance. At the end he reached the point of striking out for a full free-church system. Williams, concluded Cotton Mather, struck at "the whole political, as well as ecclesiastical constitution of the country."

The vigorous liberalism of these agitations, the support they won from the people in Salem, and the penalty they brought show the subtle relevance of the system of banishments to the political purposes of the governing class. Thomas Shepard issued sober warning against a principle which figured in the case of Williams: "if the magistrate hath no power over his subjects in matters of the first table he may have also all his feathers pull'd from him." It is scarcely conceivable that on October 9 when Williams stood before them, the magistrates were unmindful of Shepard's point.

"Liberty of searching out Truth," said Williams in a later great appeal for freedom, is "hardly got, and as hardly kept." For that precious "Jewel," New England had run mighty hazards; but if New England forgot the nature of liberty, if it made it "a crime, humbly and peaceably to question even Lawes and Statutes, or what ever is even publickly taught and delivered," then it would find itself enslaved and in "Chains," a captive of ignorance and dark superstition. Roger Williams' fear stemmed from an accurate perception of the historic transformation of overseas Puritanism. The founding of New England set the stage for a subtle sea change. From constitutional resistance to the absolutism of the Stuarts and the innovations of Laud, the Puritan fathers moved backward into the bleak pathway of arrogant domination.

In 1676 the general court thought sufficiently better of Williams to grant him a temporary suspension of banishment. Three centuries after the trial the proud commonwealth of Massachusetts did an intended honor to Rhode Island by officially rescinding the sentence against Williams—and in the same year passed a teachers' oath, backtracking toward 1600! For some years, by that time, the state of which Roger Williams was the original founder had had a red-hot teachers' oath of its own.

Edmund S. Morgan: THE PURITAN DILEMMA: THE STORY OF JOHN WINTHROP

Most historians in the first half of the twentieth century had found their heroes especially among those who, like Williams, had questioned or opposed the established authorities. As scholarship widened our knowledge of the historical context, as Americans found themselves faced with the responsibilities of world power and the challenge of Communism, more and more historians after 1950 turned their attention to leaders who had exercised power responsibly and to thinkers who had recognized the dangers in utopianism. Edmund Morgan's biography of John Winthrop, published in 1958, presented a view of the Puritan leaders and of Williams's controversy with them which differed considerably from the picture drawn by Parrington and Brockunier.

A SPECIAL COMMISSION

TO please God the Puritans demanded of themselves a standard of behavior not far different from that required by most modern codes of morality. They did not think it necessary to be either prudes or prohibitionists. They did not dress in drab clothes or live in drab houses or speak in drab words. The people who appear in the pages of Winthrop's journal, the good men and women who showered him with venison and partridges and fat hogs to celebrate Margaret's arrival, the boys and girls who skipped rope on the decks of the *Arbella,* the men who built ships and caught fish and planted corn were all human enough.

Nevertheless, the Puritans did make strong demands on human nature, for they were engaged in a mission that required great exertion. They had undertaken to establish a society where the will of God would be observed in every detail, a kingdom of God on earth. While still aboard the *Arbella,* Winthrop had explained to his fellow emigrants their solemn commitment to this task. Every nation, they all knew, existed by virtue of a covenant with God in which it promised to obey His commands. They had left England because England was failing in its promise. In high hope that God was guiding them and would find their efforts acceptable, they had proposed to form a new society. Now God had demonstrated His approval. He had made way for them by a "special overruling providence." By staying His wrath so long and allowing them to depart in peace, by delivering them safe across the water, He had sealed a covenant with them and given them a special responsibility to carry out the good intentions that had brought them into the wilderness. Theirs was a special commission. And "when God gives a special Commission," Winthrop warned them, "He lookes to have it stricktly observed in every Article."

All must therefore work together to attain the end of their coming. They must not allow any selfish private motives to interfere with their plan, for though every society must make its covenant with God, they had been singled out, like Israel of old, to serve as a model for others. They would be a city set on a hill: "the eies of all people are uppon us; soe that if wee shall deal falsely with our god in this worke wee have undertaken and soe cause him to withdrawe his present help from us, wee shall be made a story and a by-word through the world, wee shall open the mouthes of enemies to speake evill of the wayes of god and all professours for Gods sake; wee shall shame the faces of many of gods worthy servants, and cause theire prayers to be turned into Cursses upon us till wee be consumed out of the good land whither wee are goeing."

Winthrop was determined that Massachusetts should not deal falsely with God. Before arriving in New England, he and the other leaders of the exodus had thought long and hard about the articles of God's special commission, and they were confident that they knew what was required of them. They knew, in the most elementary terms, that they must punish every sin committed in Massachusetts. And punish they did, with the eager cooperation of the whole community, who knew that sin unpunished might expose them all to the wrath of God. Families became little cells of righteousness where the mother and father disciplined not only their children but also their servants and any boarders they might take in. In order that no one should escape this wholesome control, it was forbidden for anyone to live alone: unmarried men and maids were required to place themselves in some family if their own had been left behind. Parents were obliged to take care that all their children and apprentices learned to read, so that everyone would be able to see for himself in the Bible what opportunities for salvation God offered to man and what sins He forbade. The churches were thronged every Sunday with willing and unwilling worshipers—everyone was required to attend—and church members guarded each other's morals by censuring or excommunicating those who strayed from the straight path.

With virtually the whole population for a police force Winthrop found it no problem to punish sin. It was sometimes difficult, however, to determine exactly what was sinful and what was not. The grosser forms of sin were easily identified. Among the emigrants were men—and women too—who stole and fought and made love without a marriage contract and cursed their betters with primeval eloquence. In these cheerful practitioners sin wore obvious labels. But some cases were not so clear. The line between sin and mere temptation or between sin and simple human pleasure was often a thin one. Yet Winthrop knew that that line must be firmly drawn, for it would be as wrong to forbid what God allowed as it would be to allow what He forbade.

How easy it was to err and how earnestly the Puritans sought to avoid error may be seen in their treatment of the problem of alcohol. The Puritans did not make the simple mistake of condemning all use of alcohol. Liquor was one of the good things that God had furnished His people for their comfort, nourishment, and recreation. Drunkenness, however, was wrong, and the Puritans punished it without hesitation. But the path from drink to drunkenness was so short and easy that they found it hard to decide whether any barriers should be placed along it. Since the path seemed to be even shorter for Indians than for Englishmen, the authorities at one time forbade the sale of all liquors to them but later relented on the ground that it was "not fit to deprive the Indians of any lawfull comfort which God aloweth to all men by the use of wine." For themselves the closest the Puritans came to a self-denying ordinance was a law forbidding people to drink toasts to one another. In passing it they hoped to prevent drunkenness, quarreling, bloodshed, uncleanness, misuse of precious time—and the waste of wine and beer.

Here, in spite of the appeal to frugality, they went beyond the terms of God's commission, for they were forbidding a temptation rather than a sin. Winthrop's friend and adviser Thomas Shepard, the respected minister of the church at Cambridge, pointed out the defection. The law, said Shepard in a letter to Winthrop, was all wrong. By treating a temptation as a sin, it would provoke God, for this was making "more sins than (as yet is seene) God himselfe hath made."

In general Winthrop avoided such errors of judgment himself. But many men who had not learned the lesson he had were determined to set up more sins than God did, because they did not know the limits of man's ability and of God's commands. These well-meaning zealots failed to recognize that God's kingdom on earth must still be a kingdom of flesh and blood, and their misdirected zeal soon indicated to Winthrop that he faced a far more difficult problem to control the good than to punish the wicked.

The authorities in England, of course, had a way of handling the problem of fanatics: bore their tongues, cut off their ears, brand them, imprison them, silence them. Though all these methods were ultimately used in Massachusetts, they did not commend themselves to anyone with Winthrop's political sense. The result of their use in England was not the suppression but the multiplication of fanatics, who swarmed out of the country to Holland and to New England. (They did not leave as fast as they multiplied, however, and in ten years' time rose up to overwhelm their oppressors.)

In Massachusetts Winthrop had no intention of making the mistakes that King Charles and Bishop Laud were making in England. He welcomed all Puritans who fled from the mother country. Every ship that arrived in Boston carried its cargo of them, simple men and women for the most part, who had come with much the same purpose in mind that he had, people who had learned not to aim higher than God demanded, and not lower, either. But among them was a liberal proportion of those who did aim too high.

Some were separatists, men who had renounced the Church of England and proposed to live and worship in unblemished purity in the New World. Theirs was the position that Winthrop and his friends had expressly disavowed in the statement issued aboard the *Arbella* before departure. Others, while not separatist in name (because they failed to repudiate the Anglican Church), were nevertheless separatist by nature. They too looked for perfection in this world and had come to New England to be right while the rest of the world went wrong.

This separatist impulse was probably present to some degree in most settlers. The men who came to New England had shown, by so doing, that they were unwilling to tolerate evils that other men found tolerable. They had burned their bridges; they had lost whatever they had to lose through intransigence, and they were in consequence all the more ready to insist on their opinions, all the more reluctant to compromise. Some of them had stood before Bishop Laud and defied him. Would they hesitate to defy John Winthrop or anyone else who ventured to disagree with them?

To construct a commonwealth of such persons, a commonwealth "wherein the least known evills are not to bee tollerated," was a delicate task. Their constant demand for purity threatened in several ways the success of Winthrop's mission to the wilderness. Not only did they seek to read into the commission articles which God, in Winthrop's view at least, had not put there, but when their extravagant demands were not met, they threatened to disrupt the colony. The separatist was always ready to disagree with his neighbors and, when they failed to meet his standards, to withdraw into a lofty and querulous independence, accompanied by all whom he could persuade to join him. In a population so heavily burdened with principles as that of Massachusetts, the danger of such withdrawals was constant. And if the process once began, there was no telling where it would stop. Separatism might splinter the colony into a hundred earnest little Utopias, each feeding on its own special type of holiness and each breeding new types, multiplying, like earthworms, by division. Separatists could disintegrate the colony and dissolve its special commission.

Separatism posed another, external danger when it reached the point of repudiating the churches of England. Winthrop and most of his colleagues thought that such a repudiation would be wrong in itself, a failure of charity, an arrogation of too exclusive a righteousness. But it would also be a danger to the execution of the colony's special commission, because it might excite the anger of the English Government. If the King and his bishops heard that Massachusetts disavowed the Church of England, they might revoke the charter and put an end to the whole experiment.

This was a danger not easily met. It was impossible to censor every letter sent home, and jubilant Puritans frequently wrote back in gloating terms about the purity of their churches by comparison with the corruption of England. "You that are under lee I hope forgett us not that are yett in the storme," an English friend wrote apprehensively to Winthrop, but too many New Englanders remembered their friends in England only to vaunt it over them. Occasionally individuals would return to the mother country to settle unfinished business, and these first innocents abroad proved quite as insufferable in their claims of superior holiness as later generations in their claims of superior plumbing. As a result the colony was in continual danger of interference from England.

The history of Massachusetts during Winthrop's lifetime is very largely the history of his efforts to meet the various dangers presented by separatism. No one could have been better equipped for the task, for Winthrop was obliged to do for Massachusetts precisely what he had already done for himself. He had learned not to avoid but to face temptations, not to spurn the good things that God had given him; even so he must restrain the overzealous from setting for the community a standard of godliness that would deny the humanity of human beings. He had learned not to expect perfection in this world, and to march in company with other sinners, for sin, though it must be punished, could not be stamped out. Even so he must temper the zeal of the separatists and prevent them from splitting the community or leading it in search of impossible goals.

His success in suppressing the separatist impulse within himself was good reason for supposing that he might suppress it in Massachusetts. But he could not have foreseen how much more powerful a force separatism would prove in New England than it had in old.

In England the focal point of Puritan irritation had always been the church, and in Massachusetts the most important requirement of the colony's special commission, everyone agreed, was the establishment of churches organized precisely as God commanded. English Puritans had considered this crucial matter for three generations but had never been able to agree on what precisely God did command. They all knew there must be an end to bishops and archbishops, an end to the idolatrous ritual and trappings that exalted the clergy instead of God in the divine service, but they disagreed about two important matters.

One group, known as presbyterians, insisted that the bishops be replaced by another organization, with churches and clergy arranged in a pyramidal structure: groups of churches would be formed into presbyteries, presbyteries into synods, and these collective bodies would exercise a supervisory control over their members. The other Puritans, who ultimately took the name of Congregationalists, had a simpler plan: destroy the bishops and then let each individual church, each congregation, be sufficient to itself. There was, they said, no church larger than a congregation.

The second point on which presbyterians and congregationalists differed was the composition of the church. The presbyterians wished to continue the practice of admitting to membership and to the sacraments everyone who did not forfeit the privilege by some scandalously sinful behavior. The congregationalists, on the other hand, insisted that membership be confined to persons who could prove, beyond a reasonable doubt, that they had been singled out by God for salvation. It was possible to tell who was a saint, they thought, even in this world, and while everyone must be made to attend church, only the saints should be admitted to membership.

The congregationalists thus wished to make more sweeping changes than the presbyterians. Some of them were so impatient with the Church of England that they did not wait for the opportunity to change it but simply withdrew and formed their own churches. These were the separatists already noticed. Restriction of membership and local independence made it possible to begin a congregational church anywhere that a handful of saints could be gathered for the purpose. Indeed, one of the men who first expounded the system called it "reformation without tarrying for any," a phrase which adequately states the aim of separatists in all ages.

In the mass migration of the 1630's many separatists came and doubtless many presbyterians, but the leaders and probably the majority of immigrants were congregationalists who had declined to repudiate the English churches. Because they had refused to separate, they had had no previous practical experience in the operation of congregationalism and, with a very few exceptions, knew it only from books. Winthrop, for example, had been the patron of the church at Groton, with power to appoint the minister there. It is possible that he allowed the congregation to make the choice, according to congregational precept, and it is likely that the Groton church was very lax about conforming to the prescribed rituals of the Church of England, but there could have been no exclusion of the unregenerate from membership. Consequently, neither Winthrop nor any of the other Puritans, who came from similar situations, could have appreciated in advance what forces would be released and what problems created by the wholesale practice of congregationalism.

The first church within the boundaries of Massachusetts Bay to be founded in the congregational manner was "gathered" (the term usually employed) on July 20, 1629, at Salem by the settlers sent out under Endecott. As the great wave of men and women arrived the following year, they followed the instructions in their books and gathered churches as rapidly as they dug themselves in. By 1635 a dozen churches were scattered round the bay from Hingham to Newbury.

At its beginning a church contained only a handful of members. Usually it was thought proper to start with at least seven, though at Charlestown there were only four. The first members chose a minister and began the process of sifting the population of their town, or "plantation." As every candidate for membership appeared, they satisfied themselves of his sainthood. He was obliged to describe the whole course of his previous life, explain how he reached the moment of conversion, and show how his subsequent life had exhibited its effects. If he passed this examination, he was allowed to subscribe the church covenant, by which he agreed to join with the other members in worship and holy living. Having done so, he then participated in the judgment of future candidates. Generally a unanimous consent was required for every admission.

For ten years the human flood swept into Massachusetts, pushing up the rivers, swarming over the champion lands, some twenty thousand souls, and every soul was checked off as saved or damned. The effect on those who failed to make the grade is difficult to calculate. Some were doubtless conscientious Puritans who simply never felt the moving of grace in their souls and did not want admission without it. Others may have been hardened sinners who scorned admission on any terms, men who could wield a hammer and a spade and a tankard and curse the godly with a free heart. Whoever they were they made surprisingly few complaints about exclusion from the privileges of church membership.

The effect on the saints, however, was profound. They were required continually to pass judgment of the most dreadful kind on their fellow men. They must search not only their own souls for signs of grace, but the souls of their neighbors. As they gathered together in their pure churches, placing the mark of holiness on their own foreheads and of damnation on most of their neighbors, the experience could not fail to induce that intellectual arrogance which is the breeder of separatism. Though in England they had denounced the evils of separation, the very act of forming a congregational church necessitated an assumption of superior purity and thereby encouraged a separatist frame of mind. Never in American history did a community produce separatists more attractive or more dangerous than those of early Massachusetts.

What made them dangerous was that the congregationalism which propagated them also blocked the most obvious means of controlling them. Both in the

Church of England and in the presbyterian system a central organization could police the orthodoxy of individual churches. Congregationalism allowed no central organization: every church was independent. Thus while one distinctive feature of congregationalism, regenerate membership, encouraged separatism, another feature, congregational autonomy, destroyed the most effective method of control. The people of Massachusetts had in fact undertaken an almost impossible task: they had accepted a commission which required them to follow a specific body of religious principles; but among those principles was one which encouraged the development of schism and another which denied them the means of preventing it.

The Puritans tried always to rest their religious principles, like their social, political, legal, and moral ones, on the Bible, the infallible guidebook for establishing a kingdom of God on earth. But the Bible, while it spoke with unquestioned authority, said different things to different men. To some it seemed to prescribe presbyterianism, to others congregationalism, and to different congregationalists it said different things about baptism or sanctification or communion. The congregationalists who founded New England were pretty well agreed on what it said about most matters, but among so many earnest students of the Bible, there was always one to discover a new and heretical meaning in a familiar passage and to demand that everyone else accept it. More often than not the innovator was a minister who used his pulpit to persuade his congregation, and the separatist impulse would soon be threatening to split that congregation away from the rest of the colony. With congregational independence recognized as a fundamental principle, what was to prevent it?

Fortunately, reason could heal differences as well as create them, and the Puritans were extraordinarily reasonable men. The zeal with which they studied the Bible sprang from supreme confidence in the ability of reason to find the truth there. Not knowledge but ignorance, they believed, was the mother of heresy. Therefore they listened with respect to every man who could give reasons for his opinions, and if they thought his reasons faulty, they used every possible argument to persuade him. The paper relics of their contests have survived: the arguments and the answers to arguments and the replies to the answers and the answers to the replies to the answers, all loaded with scriptural citations. It was a tedious process, but usually it worked, because these people feared to err and took each other seriously.

Because they were so reasonable they were also able to do much by informal methods. The clergy were all learned men, skilled in marshaling arguments, and enjoyed therefore a social and intellectual prestige that enabled them to exert a powerful influence among their people—so powerful that New England congregationalism came to be known as a speaking aristocracy in the face of a silent democracy. Though they were excluded from authority beyond their respective congregations, the handicaps of congregational independence were minimized when the ministers of a particular locality began meeting together in "consociations" to thrash out disagreements. If the ministers could agree, the congregations would be likely to. When an especially difficult problem arose, it was possible to call a synod, not of course the presbyterian type of synod with authority to establish its findings, but a congregational synod, which was simply a full meeting of the colony's ministers, whose findings had no more authority than the report of a committee of experts called in for consultation. No individual or church was obliged to abide by the report, but most pious men and women would hesitate to back their own views above the collective wisdom of the clergy.

Much could be done by such indirect methods to keep individuals and churches from flying off on separatist tangents. But in the end there had to be some tribunal, some court of last resort, to deal with the man or church that had gone too far in separatism to listen to argument. Since each congregation could rightfully claim an absolute independence of the others, such a tribunal could not lie with the churches or with their clergy. But what was forbidden to the church was not necessarily forbidden to the state. The state was charged with the colony's commission. The state was responsible for suppressing heresy as well as drunkenness and theft and murder. In the hands of the state's government, then, lay the final, supreme responsibility. And John Winthrop came to Massachusetts as the head of that government. He had scarcely arrived when he began a series of moves to make of it a simple but effective instrument for controlling separatism and maintaining a colony united in the execution of God's commission.

A DUE FORM OF GOVERNMENT

When Winthrop and eleven other members of the Massachusetts Bay Company met at Cambridge, England, on August 26, 1629, they agreed to go to New England if the charter and headquarters of the company could be transferred with them. Ten of the twelve kept their pledge, eight of them arriving with Winthrop or shortly after. Besides these, Winthrop could count only four or five other members of the company in New England at the end of 1630. This handful of men was now the Massachusetts Bay Company and endowed with all the powers described in the charter which Winthrop guarded among his papers.

In the charter the King had granted authority "to make, ordeine, and establishe all manner of wholesome and reasonable orders, lawes, statutes, and ordinances, directions, and instructions, not contrarie to the lawes of this our realm of England, as well for setling of the forms and ceremonies of government and magistracy fitt and necessary for the said plantation, and the inhabitants there, and for nameing and stiling of all sortes of officers, both superior and inferior, which they shall finde needeful for that governement and plantation, and the distinguishing and setting forth of the severall duties, powers, and lymytts of every such office and place."

It was intended, of course, that these extensive powers should be exercised by a corporation meeting in England; but the charter did not say so, and the only actual limitation which the King placed on the company's governmental authority over Massachusetts Bay was that it should make no laws repugnant to the laws of England. Settlers going to the colony from England and their children born there were to enjoy "all liberties and immunities" that they would have had if they had been born in England. But English birth did not in 1630 confer the right to participate in government, and the charter did not specify that the consent of the settlers should be obtained for the laws made to govern them. Instead the company had full powers to legislate for the colony and to organize a government to carry out their decrees in any way they saw fit.

With regard to the organization and government of the company itself the charter was much more specific. The members, known as "freemen," were to meet four times a year in a "Great and General Court," to make laws for both company and colony. Once a year, at one of these courts, they would elect a governor, a deputy governor, and eighteen "assistants" for the coming year, to manage affairs between meetings of the General Court. This executive council was to meet every month. The governor or deputy governor and at least six of the assistants must be present also at every meeting of the General Court, but the charter did not specify that any other members must be present to constitute a quorum, so that these seven officers, in the absence of any other members, could presumably exercise all the powers of the General Court.

In Massachusetts, therefore, Winthrop and the dozen or so members of the company who came with him had unlimited authority to exercise any kind of government they chose over the other settlers. In order to satisfy the terms of the charter they had only to meet once a month as assistants (all but one of the members who are known to have migrated the first year were assistants) and four times a year as a General Court, though the two types of meeting would now be virtually indistinguishable in membership. Provided they followed this procedure and passed no laws repugnant to the laws of England, they could govern Massachusetts in any way they saw fit. And for that matter, who was to say what law was repugnant to those of England? Who was to decide, who to correct them if they erred? Here was no King, Parliament, bishop, or judge to stand in their way.

A group of men as sure of their cause as were Winthrop and his friends must have been strongly tempted to establish themselves as a permanent aristocracy or oligarchy, holding fast the power granted in the charter and using it to enforce the special commission which they believed God had given them. They were a determined, stiff-jawed set, quick to anger and slow to laughter, as likely a group of oligarchs as ever assembled. John Endecott and Thomas Dudley, after Winthrop the most influential of the group, were also the most headstrong.

Endecott had been governing the colony under instructions from the company in England before Winthrop and the others got there. Winthrop saw no need for any such subordinate officer after his own arrival on the scene, but Endecott was still a member of the company and entitled to a place in its councils. He was a soldier by past experience and by temperament, impatient of civilian impertinence, all too ready to draw his sword or strike out with a fist when his commands were not obeyed with alacrity. The General Court commissioned him to keep the peace in Salem, where he continued to live, but his notion of keeping the peace was sometimes far from peaceful. On one occasion, when a man had not treated him with due respect, he felt obliged to defend his dignity with his fists. When Winthrop rebuked him, he answered, "I acknowledge I was too rash in strikeing him, understanding since that it is not lawfull for a justice of peace to strike. But if you had seene the manner of his carriadge, with such daring of mee with his armes on kembow etc. It would have provoked a very patient man." And this John Endecott was not.

Neither was Thomas Dudley, who as deputy governor was Winthrop's second-in-command. Dudley was a rigid, literal-minded type, ready to exact his pound of flesh whenever he thought it due him. As steward of the Earl of Lincoln in England he had prided himself on getting the Earl out of debt by raising the tenants' rents. In Massachusetts he engrossed quantities of corn and lent it to his poorer neighbors on credit, to receive ten bushels for seven and a half after harvest. Winthrop regarded this practice as oppressive usury, but Dudley's temper flared when his conduct was questioned in any way. He was obviously not the sort of man to diminish his own authority.

Winthrop himself was more mature than Dudley or Endecott would ever be. His long struggle with his passions had left him master of himself in a way that few men ever achieve. The fire was still there, and if blown up by other men's wrath, it would occasionally burst out, but generally it lay well below the surface, imparting a warmth and power which everyone around him sensed. Winthrop, as he himself realized, had acquired a talent for command. He never grasped for authority as Dudley or Endecott might, but he did not need to: he was the kind of man upon whom authority was inevitably thrust.

These three men, all disposed in their different ways to command those around them, were equipped also with a philosophy of government to give their commands a superhuman sanction. For more than a hundred years Protestants had been confronting the pope with declarations of the God-given authority of civil rulers. In England Anglican and Puritan alike maintained the divine right of their king against the enemy at Rome, who claimed a power to depose Protestant monarchs. Though the Puritans reserved to the people a right of resistance against tyrants who violated the laws of God, they were always ready to quote the Epistle to the Romans in support of rulers who enforced the laws of God. And the members of the Massachusetts Bay Company were all godly men; they had come with no other intention than to see God's will done at last.

Winthrop never lost an opportunity to affirm his belief that the powers that be were ordained of God and must be honored and respected accordingly. While still aboard the *Arbella*, he had reminded the other passengers that "God Almightie in his most holy and wise providence hath soe disposed of the Condicion of mankinde, as in all times some must be rich some poore, some highe and eminent in power and dignitie; others meane and in subjeccion." There was no doubt in Winthrop's mind that God intended civil governments to be in the hands of men like himself; to entrust the people at large with powers of government, as in a Greek democracy, was not only unwarranted by Scripture but dangerous to the peace and well-being of the community, for the people at large were unfit to rule. The best part of them was always the smallest part, "and of that best part the wiser part is always the lesser."

Winthrop and the other members of the Bay Company were authorized by their charter to exercise absolute powers of government; they were endowed by temperament with the inclination to exercise those powers; and they were assisted by a philosophy of government which clothed every civil ruler in the armor of divine authority. How natural, then, that they should become a ruling oligarchy. They might readily have succumbed to the lust for power, since power lay unchallenged in their hands.

But they did not succumb.

They did not even keep the powers to which the charter entitled them.

After Winthrop had explored the bay and moved the headquarters of the colony from Salem to Charlestown, he summoned the assistants for their first meeting on August 23, 1630. There were seven members present besides himself and Dudley, and they got down to the business of government at once. They provided for the maintenance of two ministers, set maximum wages for workmen in various trades, and appointed a beadle "to attend upon the Governor, and alwaies to be ready to execute his commands in publique businesses." They also ordered that there should be regular meetings, or "courts," of the assistants and of the General Court, though the difference between the two would be a formality, since their membership would be virtually identical (unless future emigration brought over other company members without the status of assistant). On September 7 and September 28 they met again as assistants and exercised their authority in a variety of actions. They forbade the sale of firearms to the Indians; they put an embargo on corn; they seized Richard Clough's strong water because he sold too much of it to other men's servants; and they fined Sir Richard Saltonstall, one of their own number, for being absent from court.

Then on October 19 Winthrop summoned at Charlestown the first meeting labeled in the records as a General Court. For this day he and the seven company members who met with him had prepared a revolution that was to affect the history of Massachusetts from that time forward. The records described the event with tantalizing brevity: "For the establishinge of the government. It was propounded if it were not the best course that the Freemen should have the power of chuseing Assistants when there are to be chosen, and the Assistants from amongst themselves to chuse a Governor and Deputy Governor, whoe with the Assistants should have the power of makeing lawes and chuseing officers to execute the same."

This was surely a strange proposal to make to a group of men all of whom were both freemen and assistants. Why, when there were no freemen but themselves in the colony, should they make provision for freemen electing the assistants and the assistants electing the other officers? One begins to get an inkling of what was happening in the next sentence of the records: "This was fully assented unto by the generall vote of the people, and ereccion of hands."

The "people" here referred to were not simply the eight company members present. This we can conclude from events that followed. Winthrop had apparently thrown open the first meeting of the General Court to the whole body of settlers assembled at Charlestown. Together they had established the first constitution of Massachusetts. It used the terminology of the charter, and presumably allowed the provisions of the charter not expressly revised to remain in effect. But by general vote of the people of Massachusetts, the assistants were transformed from an executive council into a legislative assembly; and the term "freeman" was transformed from a designation for the members of a commercial company, exercising legislative and judicial control over that company and its property, into a designation for the citizens of a state, with the right to vote and hold office. The right of the citizen freemen to vote, however, was confined to electing assistants. These assistants, and not the freemen themselves, were to make laws and appoint from their own number a governor and deputy governor.

This transformation of the Bay Company's charter into a constitution for government of the colony would scarcely have been necessary or desirable if the members of the company had intended to keep control in their own hands. The reduction of the freemen's role in the government and the securing of popular consent to this change presaged the admission to freemanship of a large proportion of settlers, men who could contribute to the joint stock nothing but godliness and good citizenship. The transformation of trading company into commonwealth was completed at the next meeting of the General Court, when one hundred and sixteen persons were admitted as freemen. (This was probably most, if not all, of the adult males, excluding servants, then in the colony.) The new freemen then voted that elections should be annual and, doubtless at the behest of Winthrop, that "for time to come noe man shalbe admitted to the freedome of this body polliticke, but such as are members of some of the churches within the lymitts of the same." Though stated in the form of a limitation, this declaration was in fact an open invitation to every future church member in Massachusetts to take up the privileges of freemanship.

Since the people had no political rights under the charter, Winthrop had given them a role to which they had had no legal claim at all. That he confined the gift to church members was not surprising: he would scarcely have wished to take into partnership all of the multitude of men who might come to his colony for the wrong reasons, and the qualified franchise might also help attract the right kind of settlers. By limiting freemanship to church members he extended political rights to a larger proportion of the people than enjoyed such rights in England—and to people who were better qualified to use them than the mere possessors of a forty-shilling freehold. The question that needs to be answered is not why he limited suffrage but why he extended it. What induced Winthrop and the other members of the Bay Company to resign voluntarily the exclusive powers which the charter conferred on them and which their political beliefs and native dispositions made congenial?

Possibly they gave way to popular demand, but there is no evidence that any such demand existed. Possibly they felt a need to keep their own ranks filled. With sickness and death whittling away at their number, they were already close to the minimum quota of seven assistants required by the charter for the holding of the Assistants Court (only six were required in the General Court). But granting their need to perpetuate themselves, they could still have filled vacancies with a few hand-picked men as the need arose. The charter gave them express permission to admit new members to the company if they chose, but it put them under no obligation to do so. Even a popular demand, if it existed, could have been met by a less drastic measure than the one they took.

The real answer as to why they opened the door to freemanship so wide is to be found in the terms of the commission with which they believed the colony was entrusted. The idea of a "covenant," or contract, between God and man occupied a pre-eminent place in their thought: it was the basis of an individual's salvation; it was the origin of every true church and also of every state. "It is of the nature and essence of every society," Winthrop once wrote, "to be knitt together by some Covenant, either expressed or implyed." God's special commission to Massachusetts was an implied covenant.

But there was more than one covenant involved in the establishment of any society. After the people joined in covenant with God, agreeing to be bound by his laws, they must establish a government to see those laws enforced, for they did not have enough virtue to carry out their agreement without the compulsive force of government. They must decide among themselves what form of government they wanted and then create it by a voluntary joint compact—a second covenant.

Winthrop evidently thought that the mere act of coming to Massachusetts constituted a sufficient acceptance of the basic covenant, the special commission which God had given the colony. But the second covenant, establishing the government, required a more explicit agreement. Though the King's charter gave the Bay Company a clear and exclusive right to govern the territory, the King's authority was insufficient. The "due form of government" which Winthrop believed the special commission called for could originate only from a covenant between the settlers and the men who were to rule them. Hence the extraordinary action of October 19, with its sequel, the extension of freemanship.

Winthrop did not believe that in extending freemanship he had transformed Massachusetts into a democracy. The legislative power was lodged not in the people but in a select group where, according to his reading of the Bible, it belonged. Nor was Winthrop's action in securing the consent of the people to his government an affirmation of the principle that governments derive their just powers from the consent of the governed. He did not believe that the officers chosen under the new system would be simply the agents of the people who elected them. Rulers, however selected, received their authority from God, not from the people, and were accountable to God, not to the people. Their business was to enforce the nation's covenant with God, and during their term of office, so long as they devoted themselves to this business, they were free to act as they thought best, suiting their actions to the circumstances.

Winthrop did believe that the people, or a properly qualified portion of them, were entitled to determine the form of government to be established over them and to select the persons who should run that government. These two operations performed, their role was played out until, under the form of government they had chosen, it was time to elect new rulers. If a ruler failed in his duty to enforce the laws of God, the people would be obliged to turn him out without waiting for election time. But so long as he did his duty, his authority was absolute, and, regardless of any errors of judgment he might make, the people were obliged to submit. Indeed, anything less than submission would be rebellion against the authority of God.

In Winthrop's view, then, he had not in any way limited or reduced the authority of government by extending to church members a voice in the selection of the men who were to exercise the authority. Rather he had given to government a practical strength which it could not otherwise have possessed, for Winthrop was enough of a politician to know that, regardless of any divine authority a ruler might claim, people would submit to him more readily if they had a voice in choosing him, especially a Puritan people well educated by their ministers in the principle of government based on covenant.

There was a danger, of course, that the people would choose the wrong kind of men to rule them. Government was a difficult business, not something that one honest man could do as well as another. It required not only virtue but learning and wisdom as well: learning because the laws of God were not so obvious that he who runs might read them, wisdom because the ruler must be able to apply the laws every day to new situations and choose the right law for the case in hand. But the limitation of freemanship to church members furnished some insurance against the wiles of demagogues. Winthrop counted on the ministers to give the people sound advice and to instruct them about the kind of men who were best fitted to rule.

The ministers must not seek public office themselves, and there was little likelihood that they would or that they would succeed if they did. Though the ministers enjoyed a powerful influence over their congregations, the shadow of Rome still lay heavily on the Puritans. None of them wanted a "theocracy" in the sense of a government by the clergy. Indeed, of all the governments in the Western world at the time, that of early Massachusetts gave the clergy least authority. As long as Winthrop lived, ministers neither sought nor obtained government office. Their advice was frequently asked and frequently given; their influence over the people was invaluable; but authority rested firmly in the hands of laymen.

Under the new constitution Winthrop and most of the original assistants were re-elected until 1634. With the explicit consent of the new body of freemen and the support of the ministers, they moved swiftly and with assurance to establish in Massachusetts the kind of society that God's commission called for. The offense which they dealt with most severely was contempt of their God-given authority. The New World, with a three-thousand-mile moat on the one hand and boundless free land on the other, offered strong temptation to adventurous spirits to kick over the traces and defy every kind of authority. The American frontiersman with his fine scorn for the restrictions of civilization had not yet emerged, but he had his prototype in men like Maverick and Blackstone, who had thought Massachusetts Bay a good enough place before the saints arrived to purify it. A number of such men were on hand when the Great Migration began, and more came with it. If the Puritan experiment was to succeed, they would have to be kept strictly in check or else removed. Blackstone removed himself to the Narragansett country, remarking that he had left England because he did not like the Lord Bishops and found the rule of the Lord Brethren no better. Maverick remained behind but moved to the comparative isolation of Noddle's Island, where his bibulous hospitality frequently annoyed the government. Others, less discreet than these two, got themselves whipped and fined and banished. John Stone, for example, the captain of a small pinnace, was suspected of adultery, and his vessel was stayed until the matter could be investigated, whereupon he went to Roger Ludlow, one of the justices, and called him "just ass." This kind of punning was dangerous, and though a grand jury could not find enough evidence to indict him for adultery, he was given a suspended fine of a hundred pounds for his contempt of authority and ordered not to enter the colony again without permission on pain of death.

In operating their new government, Winthrop and the assistants did not differentiate sharply between judicial and legislative functions. Guided by the laws of God as set down in the Bible and fortified with the absolute authority to enforce those laws in any way they saw fit, they felt little need for explicit legislation. They needed no law, for example, to tell them that Mr. Clearke was looking too longingly at the mistress of the family in which he lived, Mrs. Freeman, "concerning whome there is stronge suspicion on incontinency"; they simply forbade Mr. Clearke to live with the Freemans or to keep company with Mrs. Freeman. Nor did they need any special law to justify their punishment of Nicholas Knopp by a fine of five pounds "for takeing upon him to cure the scurvey by a water of noe worth nor value, which hee solde att a very deare rate." Since adultery, which was punishable by death under the Biblical code, had seldom been punished in England at all, the court did legislate explicitly on that subject, providing the punishment God demanded. But for the most part their general orders dealt with prudential matters, such as the times for burning land to clear it, the cutting of timber, the fixing of bounties on wolves, the fencing of corn, and the disposal of straying cattle and swine.

Because they were free to act without restraint, by enjoining good actions as well as punishing bad ones they could keep a sharp watch on every kind of heresy and nip ill weeds in the bud. They could argue men out of dangerous positions before an impasse was reached, and doubtless the effectiveness of their arguments owed much to the fact that the authority of the state could enforce them if necessary.

The way Winthrop operated this government and the kind of problem he had to deal with are both well illustrated in a case that arose in 1631 in Watertown, where Winthrop's former neighbor, George Phillips, was pastor. Phillips, about a year after he and Winthrop arrived together on the *Arbella*, voiced the opinion that not only the churches of England but those of Rome too were true churches, and he succeeded in convincing many of his congregation. This was separatism inverted: the Reformation had been put through on the assumption that the Catholic Church was incurable, was no true church; it was too late now to give up the Reformation. Winthrop went to Watertown and debated before the congregation against Phillips and Richard Brown, the ruling elder (a lay officer). All but three of the liberals concluded that their opinion was an error.

Richard Brown was one of the three, an intransigent liberal. The Watertown church, probably under Winthrop's influence, formally condemned Brown's too charitable view of Catholicism but did not proceed against him for holding it. He was not even removed from office as ruling elder. The church evidently did not consider this a fatal error, and no doubt Winthrop agreed with them.

A few months later, however, another troublesome party arose in the congregation. Since Elder Brown held an erroneous opinion, some of the members felt they could not pollute themselves by remaining as communicants in the same church with him. This was a more serious matter. Again Winthrop hurried off to Watertown and this time persuaded the purists that they were going too far. There was a general reconciliation; but one John Masters, the leader of the purist faction, apparently had second thoughts afterwards and still refused to take communion with Brown, turning his back whenever the service was performed. Masters, by his exclusiveness, was committing a very serious mistake, for when he steadfastly refused to reform, the church placed its most severe penalty, excommunication, on him, after which he came round and was restored.

This incident epitomized the problem that Winthrop had wrestled with and conquered in his own life and now faced as governor. Because he had learned so painfully and so well that there was no honorable escape from the sins and perils and temptations of the world, he determined from the beginning that New England must not be an escape. The position taken by John Masters pointed straight toward escape. It could lead to the ultimate absurdity of complete withdrawal into oneself, nobody being quite pure enough to join with. It would not only separate New England from the rest of the world but split it into a host of little communities, each repudiating the others as insufficiently holy.

The position taken by Richard Brown, on the other hand, was equally dangerous to God's commission, for it led to moral indifference, to the obliteration of the distinction between Catholic and Protestant, which for Winthrop was as much as to say the distinction between right and wrong. Neither position could be allowed, but Winthrop sensed that the colony had more to fear from Masters's error than from Brown's. The most dangerous tendency among the saints of Massachusetts was not excessive liberality but excessive purity. In either case the solution lay in early and flexible treatment. Winthrop caught the danger before it got out of hand, and he did not have to prosecute anyone. The members of the church had been reasonable. After he argued them round, they handled the problem themselves.

This was the way to deal with men who wanted to be too good, and the form of government he had established gave him the maximum freedom to deal with them in this way. Absolute authority, resting on a consent that was renewed every year—this was the formula to keep zealots and scamps alike under control.

But the happy combination, happy at least in Winthrop's eyes, was not to last.

LENIENCY REBUKED

The great advantage of the government which Winthrop established in Massachusetts was its simplicity. Though it kept contact with the people by annual elections, it was otherwise a despotism with all the efficiency of despotism. It could move with speed when speed was needed and slowly when it was not. It could be lenient or severe as the occasion indicated. No cumbersome political machinery carried the governors helplessly this way or that against their wills, and no complicated body of laws dictated their decisions in every instance.

These advantages counted for much in a new colony in a new world, where preconceived rules would be constantly rubbing against unforeseen difficulties. But despotism, with all its advantages, can never be more efficient or more just or more intelligent than its despots. In the first three elections under the constitution of 1630 the freemen re-elected all the men who had held office before. The success of the government thus depended to a large degree on the abilities of Winthrop, Dudley, Endecott, and the original members of the company.

Winthrop was well equipped to exercise the powers he enjoyed. Patient, conscientious, firm but not arbitrary, he was the very soul of discretion. But he had his shortcomings. Surrounded by some of England's most brilliant young theologians, he was not himself a brilliant thinker. He was prone to take a position, perhaps intuitively, and then support it in lawyerlike fashion by every conceivable argument, even by arguments inconsistent with one another. He could see too easily the hand of God operating in his favor whenever his opponents met with some misfortune, and he took a morbid satisfaction in such events. Though he was not a vindictive man, he was distressingly fond of saying "I told you so" whenever his advice was rejected and things went wrong.

If Winthrop himself had such faults, the magistrates who were elected to serve with him (the deputy governor and the assistants) had others of a kind most unsuitable to anyone entrusted with such extensive powers. To be worthy of their authority they had to know when to be strict and when to be lenient, when to sacrifice purity to charity, when to insist and when to wheedle. They had to know how to be Puritans without being doctrinaire. The two magistrates who still carried the most weight, next to Winthrop, did not know any of these things.

Endecott unfortunately combined a hasty temper with a tendency to carry all beliefs to their logical conclusions or absurdities. In 1633 he happened to be present at a lecture in Boston when the speaker, the Reverend John Cotton, was asked whether women ought to wear veils in church. This was one of those details about which conscientious Puritans were likely to become too concerned. Cotton considered the question and concluded that veils were not necessary. Endecott was on his feet at once to argue that they were. Winthrop records with his usual economy that "after some debate, the governour, perceiving it to grow to some earnestness, interposed, and so it brake off." Endecott was just the man to make an issue out of women's veils, and the following year he all but turned the colony upside down by publicly cutting the cross out of the royal flag.

There was, however, an attractive impetuosity about Endecott, a warmth that made his shortcomings easy to forgive. Dudley, who occupied a more important position, was a colder man, with a simplicity that was far from attractive. His insistence on the last jot and tittle of the law prevailed not only where he pleaded his own cause, but in every case that came before him. On one occasion in 1633 Winthrop and the assistants were drafting an answer to an accusation made against them in England by one of the ne'er-do-wells they had shipped back there. Dudley refused to subscribe to the statement, because, in repeating the words of the accusation, the statement referred to the bishops as "reverend bishops" and also designated the King as his "sacred majesty" and professed a common belief in Christianity with the churches of England. Thomas Dudley had subscribed the Humble Request aboard the *Arbella*, but the New World was affecting him as it affected others: he now thought it would pollute him to recognize the Anglican Church.

This was precisely the kind of belligerent precisionism that Winthrop hoped to overcome by keeping the government unencumbered with rules and formalities. But how could he overcome separatism when the government itself had become infested with it? As might be expected, Winthrop's relations with Dudley were none too happy, and Dudley, more than any other single individual, frustrated the scheme of government which Winthrop had inaugurated in the meeting of October, 1630.

Part of the trouble was personal, and Winthrop may have been as much at fault as Dudley. During the early part of the first winter in New England the assistants had decided to build their houses at Cambridge (then called Newtown) and make that the capital of the colony. Accordingly Winthrop and Dudley began construction. But it became obvious as the months passed that Boston made a more convenient site than Cambridge. Winthrop seems never to have occupied his house and eventually took it down. Perhaps Dudley could not afford to do the same or to build a second house. In any case he stayed in Cambridge and felt that Winthrop treated him badly by not becoming his neighbor. Nor did Winthrop improve matters any when he told Dudley "that he did not well to bestow such cost about wainscotting and adorning his house, in the beginning of a plantation."

The difficulty between the two men was more than personal. Dudley not only lacked the discretion that Winthrop thought important in a magistrate; he disagreed that discretion was important or desirable. Dudley, as deputy governor, was close enough to the throne to be piqued at not occupying it; and the fact that he had been maneuvered into a settlement away from the center of things probably made him particularly sensitive to anything that looked like a neglect of his own office. Winthrop, it seemed to him, was exceeding his authority by taking independent action in matters that were the business of the Assistants Court.

The manner of Winthrop's defection, in Dudley's eyes, lay in being not severe enough. He was too easy on offenders, too lenient, failing to have punishments fully executed, failing to levy fines as strictly as he should. When men were banished from the colony by order of the court, he had allowed them to linger on for weeks at a time before finally expelling them. He had lent twenty-eight pounds of gunpowder to Plymouth colony without authorization. He had constructed a fort at Boston. He had let the people of Watertown build a weir on the Charles River. All these actions Dudley interpreted as a bid for popularity. Winthrop, he thought, was playing the demagogue and extending his own power at the expense of the deputy governor and assistants.

Dudley made his charges honestly to Winthrop's face at a meeting where several ministers were present; and Winthrop answered them all. The fort had been agreed upon a year before, and he had built it at his own expense. The gunpowder he had lent to Plymouth was his own, and badly needed. He had given the permission to Watertown because its people were low on provisions. If they had waited to ask permission of the court, the fishing season would have been past, "and, for his part, he would employ all his power in the court, so as he should sink under it, if it were not allowed." As for the men banished, he had power as governor to stay execution until the next meeting of the court, and he had done it because their sentence was delivered in winter: execution at once would have endangered their lives. Levying fines, he said, was the secretary's business, not his, "yet he confessed, that it was his judgment, that it were not fit, in the infancy of a commonwealth, to be too strict in levying fines, though severe in other punishments." Winthrop later admitted a general belief "that in the infancy of plantations, justice should be administered with more lenity than in a settled state, because people were then more apt to transgress, partly of ignorance of new laws and orders, partly through oppression of business and other straits."

This was a dangerous admission in a colony where the freemen were bent on observing their covenant with God. Dudley's preference for executing the laws of God with unbending rigor struck a responsive chord among the pious men and women who had seen too much lenity at home in England. Lenity meant cockfights and theaters and sports on Sunday. Lenity meant lofty prelates unrebuked by the government. Lenity meant ceremonies and rituals unwarranted by God's word. To Winthrop, of course, it meant none of these things. Yet there was a real issue here, the old issue of uncompromising purity versus charity. Winthrop, on the side of charity, sought the true course in judicial discretion rather than legislative precision.

At the same meeting where he exposed Winthrop's leniency, Dudley also attacked Winthrop on another front. At the outset he demanded to know whether Winthrop claimed authority by the charter or otherwise. By Winthrop's standards this was a blow below the belt. If he claimed authority by virtue of the constitutional agreement of the people, of October, 1630, rather than by the charter, the word would quickly go round that Massachusetts was setting up as an independent state. Such an answer would have invited trouble from England, as Dudley well knew. Winthrop dodged the question by asserting that he "would challenge no greater authority than he might by the patent." Dudley replied "that then he had no more authority than every assistant (except power to call courts, and precedency, for honor and order)." Winthrop replied that since the charter called him a governor he had whatever power belonged to a governor by common law. Angry at being forced into this position, he spoke, as he put it, "somewhat apprehensively," so that "the deputy [i.e., Deputy Governor Dudley] began to be in passion, and told the governour, that if he were so round, he would be round too. The governour bad him be round, if he would. So the deputy rose up in great fury and passion, and the governour grew very hot also, so as they both fell into bitterness."

This scene occurred on a summer's afternoon in 1632, and Winthrop's administration survived it for nearly two more years. But word of the meeting inevitably circulated, for Dudley had given the freemen a great deal to think about. Besides calling attention to Winthrop's leniency, which worried the most zealous of them, he had raised a question in their minds about the governor's authority, and they were already uneasy about the discretion Winthrop claimed and practiced. Though they could freely acknowledge that the authority of rulers came from God, Englishmen had long ago learned to fear a government that had no specific laws to restrain it. Winthrop might assure them that the Scriptures were a sufficient map to steer by, but they felt that the course should be charted and the shoals marked. And what was more, they wanted to have a hand in marking them.

The first sign that they were not altogether pleased with Winthrop's government came very early, before Dudley had made his complaint against leniency. It came from Watertown, where Pastor Phillips and Elder Brown had already brewed Winthrop one batch of trouble. He had scarcely talked the people there out of their misguided acknowledgement of Rome, when he heard that they had fallen into a more dangerous error. The government having levied a tax to build fortifications at Newtown (Cambridge), Phillips and Brown persuaded the people not to pay it, "for fear of bringing themselves and posterity into bondage."

Phillips and Brown were affirming the principle for which Winthrop's friends Sir Nathaniel Barnardiston and Sir Francis Barrington had already suffered imprisonment in England, the principle which Americans would one day follow to independence, that no taxes may be levied on a man without his consent, given in person or by his representatives. But was the principle being violated? Winthrop thought not, and the wisdom of his extension of freemanship now became apparent. Without it he would have had to tell the rebels that the charter gave absolute powers to the company, an answer that would have confirmed their fears. Instead when he summoned them before the Court of Assistants, he was able to point out, though no general election had yet taken place (only nine months had elapsed since the first new freemen were sworn in), that they had nothing to fear from a government which they themselves were entitled to elect, whereupon "they acknowledged their fault, confessing freely, that they were in an error, and made a retraction and submission under their hands."

The error of the Watertowners, Winthrop pointed out, was "that they took this government to be no other but as of a mayor and aldermen, who have not power to make laws or raise taxations without the people." If Phillips and Brown thought that the government of Massachusetts was merely that of an English borough, they did well to protest, for the mayor and aldermen who governed most English boroughs were self-perpetuating corporations, in which the people ordinarily had no share. Aldermen were elected by other aldermen whenever a death occurred in their own ranks. They also chose the mayor, usually for a one-year term, but they themselves held office for life. These petty oligarchies did not usually have the power to tax, but otherwise they enjoyed an almost absolute power within their boroughs.

The government of a borough, in other words, was very much like that which the Massachusetts Bay Company could have exercised over Massachusetts, except that the company's powers were even more extensive than those of most borough corporations. Winthrop was not using sophistry when he told the people of Watertown that the government of Massachusetts was not (he might have said "no longer") like this, that it was "rather in the nature of a parliament, and that no assistant could be chosen but by the freemen, who had power likewise to remove the assistants and put in others, and therefore at every general court (which was to be held once every year) they had free liberty to consider and propound anything concerning the same, and to declare their grievances, without being subject to question." Winthrop said, in other words, that the assistants were, like Parliament, representatives of the people, an elected body with supreme legislative and judicial authority. They were, to be sure, a small parliament, but the colony itself was small, and the ratio of representatives to population was actually a good deal larger than it was in the House of Commons.

What Winthrop failed to take into account, however, was that every assistant in Massachusetts was to be elected at large, by all the voters, not just by those of a particular locality. In England most members of the House of Commons were elected locally on local issues and served local interests while they sat in Parliament. The settlers of Massachusetts, like the Englishmen they left behind, thought of a representative, when they thought of him at all, as someone who would promote the special interests of his borough or county, someone who would know what taxes his constituents could bear and what they could not, how they would be affected by passage of this or by failure to pass that one. Winthrop's own earlier experience in Suffolk County elections should have made him aware of the value to government of men with knowledge of local conditions and needs.

Whether or not the Watertowners reminded him of this is not recorded, but ten weeks later when election time came round, the General Court ordered that two men be chosen from every plantation to confer with the governor and assistants about raising taxes. Winthrop explained why: "So as what they should agree upon should bind all." This was precisely the kind of measure he approved. Provided the representatives so chosen confined themselves to the matter of taxes, they would not interfere with the efficiency of the government, and their presence would forestall discontent.

Winthrop also agreed to another innovation at the same meeting of the General Court in 1632, namely that the election of governor and deputy governor be transferred from the assistants to the freemen. Winthrop knew in advance that the freemen were going to propose this measure and urged the assistants to accept it. Some of them were much put out. One in particular, Roger Ludlow, who later became a leading figure in Connecticut, "grew into passion and said, that then we should have no government, but there would be an interim, wherin every man might do what he pleased." Winthrop was able to reassure the rest of the assistants that the measure would bring no such disastrous consequence, but Ludlow "continued stiff in his opinion, and protested he would then return back into England." The measure passed; Ludlow remained; and the freemen re-elected Winthrop just as the assistants would have done.

Still the uneasiness about the government persisted, fed by Dudley's charges against the governor's leniency and Winthrop's admission that the authority of the government rested on the charter. Sooner or later someone would think to ask what the charter actually had to say about it. And then, inevitably, the freemen of the colony would claim as their own right all the powers that were conferred by the charter on the freemen of the original company. The word "freemen" as used in Massachusetts after 1630 meant something more and something less than was intended in the charter. The charter had used the word to designate the stockholders of the company, a body not too numerous to act as a legislative assembly. Before Winthrop extended the term to mean citizens of the colony, the settlers had consented that the term should no longer include any legislative power. If freemanship had been extended to all church members without this rule, the effect would have been to make Massachusetts a simple democracy, with hundreds of citizens gathering in some huge field to make laws. Winthrop and the other members of the company would doubtless have preferred to keep all powers in their own hands rather than establish a government of that kind. Nevertheless, since freemanship had been extended and Dudley had forced Winthrop to acknowledge the charter as the basis of government, the freemen needed only to inspect the document in order to discover that by their title they might claim a direct share in all legislation. They would certainly be disposed to make the claim, feeling as they did that legislation was needed to limit the discretion of their rulers.

The matter came to a head in the spring of 1634, when notices went out for the annual court of election to be held in May. The freemen chose a group of two men from each town to plan an agenda of other matters to be considered at this court. When these representatives met, they asked Winthrop for the charter (or "patent," as they generally called it). Upon seeing that it empowered the freemen to make laws, they asked for an explanation.

Winthrop told them that when the patent was granted, the number of freemen was small enough so that all could join in making laws. With the removal to Massachusetts and the opening of freemanship to all church members, the number became so large that it had been necessary to choose a smaller group for that purpose (he meant the assistants, who now performed all legislative, judicial, and executive functions). Perhaps in the future an additional "select company" of freemen might be designated as legislators, but the colony did not at present have "a sufficient number of men qualified for such a business." Nor could it stand the "loss of time" of so many additional men diverted from work to government. Nevertheless, he was willing to have them make a beginning at the coming General Court: they might order that once a year a certain number "be appointed (upon summons from the governour) to revise all laws, etc., and to reform what they found amiss therein; but not to make any new laws, but prefer their grievances to the court of assistants." No taxes would be levied nor any public lands disposed of without consent of this committee.

Winthrop's concessions were real, but they came too late. They still left the governor and assistants a wide discretion beyond the control of the freemen. What the freemen wanted was a full body of legislation, made by themselves or their representatives, as a guarantee against arbitrary government. Though the constitution of 1630 allowed them to elect their despots every year, they retained a healthy aversion to despotism as such, elective or hereditary, benevolent or otherwise. It was Winthrop's greatest weakness that he failed to see the merit of their view. He never ceased to think that government should be as little confined by legislation as possible.

If he had held this opinion with the same doctrinaire fervor that Endecott and Dudley displayed in less important matters, he might have lost his influence in the colony very quickly. Fortunately Winthrop's commanding position did not depend on abstract theories or legal documents. The same sense for political realities that enabled him to bring the church members into partnership in the Bay Company also enabled him to give way gracefully before popular demands when it seemed imperative to do so.

He gave way now as the freemen, following Dudley's lead, insisted on the patent as the constitution of the colony. When they met for election, they ordered that the four yearly General Courts should be held as prescribed by the patent. Realizing, however, that it would be impossible for such a large body to operate effectively, they provided that the freemen should be present only at the court for elections and at the others should send deputies from every town to act in their place, thus establishing a government in which each community had its own representatives. Winthrop was rebuked by being reduced to the rank of assistant. In his place as governor they chose Thomas Dudley, with Roger Ludlow as deputy governor, him of the hot temper who had threatened to return to England if the freemen were allowed to choose the governor and deputy governor. It is not recorded that he objected to taking office.

Winthrop accepted the change calmly; by his own political philosophy the people were entitled to determine the form of their civil government. Neither in his journal nor in his private letters did he reveal any sense of bitterness or complain of ingratitude. When the General Court demanded an account of the public expenditures during his term of office, he heaped coals of fire upon them by showing that he had frequently dipped into his own pocket to pay the bills of Massachusetts. During the next three years, while other men sat in the governor's chair, he never sulked in his tent but accepted willingly whatever small tasks were assigned him.

Winthrop was still an assistant and consequently a regular member of the General Court and the Assistants Court. In addition, people continued to come to him about matters that the new governor should have handled. Winthrop attributed this to the fact that Dudley lived in Cambridge, while his own house was conveniently located in Boston, but it was more than that. He was still John Winthrop, and his authority did not depend wholly upon votes. People might put other men in office above him, but they could never ignore the authority that Winthrop carried within him. Whoever was governor, he would still be one who governed.

SEPARATISM UNLEASHED

As long as Winthrop held the reins of government he held them lightly. Though he never hesitated to strike down sin, he was keenly aware that Massachusetts was endangered more by separatist zeal than by worldly wickedness. He knew too that the time to check separatism was early, before it became blind to every obstacle. Argument, admonition, and patience were the most effective weapons against it. Winthrop used them to such advantage that for four years, while the settlers established themselves and their churches, Massachusetts was troubled by no deep rifts between man and man.

After the freemen turned Winthrop out of the governor's chair, they filled it for the three succeeding years with men of a less flexible nature. Thomas Dudley, John Haynes, and Henry Vane were all of a kind, easily intoxicated with their own righteousness. Of John Haynes, who succeeded Dudley as governor in 1635, it is enough to say that he had joined the attack on Winthrop's leniency. Henry Vane, a more complex character, was a mere boy of twenty-three when elected to the governorship in 1636, less than a year after his arrival in Massachusetts. His father was comptroller of the King's household, and he himself had an illustrious career in England ahead of him. At this time he was full of the magnetism, the enthusiasms, and the dedication of youth. Though he had a generosity of nature that was wholly lacking in Dudley, he had the same uncompromising devotion to principle, a devotion that would bring him one day to the scaffold. He was a good man, but a dangerous one to govern a colony already overloaded with zeal.

Though Winthrop's moderation had brought the colony successfully through the crucial first years, separatism still posed a threat to its mission if not to its survival. If the rigidity of his successors should prevail, there would be great danger of crippling schisms and secessions. The Great Migration was filling Massachusetts with men and women who were not afraid to take sides and not afraid to stand up against government. Among them, as it happened, was a man named Roger Williams, a charming, sweet-tempered, winning man, courageous, selfless, God-intoxicated—and stubborn—the very soul of separatism.

Williams had been in on the Massachusetts Bay project as early as Winthrop. During the meeting at Tattershall in 1629, when Winthrop talked the whole thing out with Isaac Johnson and the others, Williams had appeared and had probably taken part in the discussions. He was a young man, fresh from Cambridge, where he had studied divinity. In 1629 he was chaplain to Sir William Masham of High Laver in Essex. Sir William was one of Winthrop's clients in the Court of Wards, and Winthrop had doubtless heard good things of Williams from him.

Williams did not depart with Winthrop and the others in the spring of 1630 but arrived the following February, in the midst of that first dreadful winter. The ship which brought him was the *Lyon*, which Winthrop had sent back for provisions the previous fall. Winthrop noted her cargo approvingly, not only the supply of lemon juice which put an end to scurvy, but also the "godly minister." He arrived at an opportune time, for the Reverend John Wilson, teacher of the Boston church, was returning to England on the *Lyon* to fetch his wife. The congregation invited Williams to officiate during his absence, and here the first premonition of trouble appeared: he refused the offer. Williams had left England with none of the reluctance that troubled Winthrop and his friends, for Williams was an avowed separatist: he felt no attachment whatever to the Church of England. In fact, since the churches of England were contaminated by the admission of unregenerate persons to communion, he could not regard them as churches at all. He had befouled himself by attending them in England; now that he was clear of them he cheerfully renounced them and repented his former weakness.

The Boston church, of course, did not admit unregenerate members. It was a true congregational church, open only to those who could prove themselves holy. But this was not enough for Williams. He could not bring himself to soil his new purity by joining in worship with people who, though pure themselves, failed to renounce the impurities of England. "I durst not," he later explained, "officiate to an unseparated people, as upon examination and conference I found them to be." Unless the members of the church would "make a public declaration of their repentance for having communion with the churches of England, while they lived there," he could not accept their offer.

Here was a separatist indeed, who would separate not only from erroneous churches but also from everyone who would not denounce erroneous churches as confidently as he did. It is not clear whether the Boston church was tempted to accept his demands, but Winthrop assuredly was not. He liked Williams, as most people did, but this sweeping repudiation of the world went against his most deeply felt convictions. He prepared a little argument to demonstrate the necessity of reforming corruption "without an absolute separation." In it he rebuked all separatists for their self-righteous denunciation of English church members as whores and drunkards. Although most Englishmen might be ignorant and misguided, he admitted, "yet whores and drunkards they are not: weake Christians they are indeed, and the weaker for want of that tender Care, that should be had of them: 1: by those that are sett over them to feede them: and next for that spirituall pride, that Sathan rooted into the hearts of their brethren, who when they are Converted, doe not, nor will not strengthen them, but doe Censure them, to be none of Gods people, nor any visible Christians."

Thus Winthrop reproached his young friend. Though Williams's opinions horrified him, it was characteristic of Winthrop to meet them with arguments and not merely with authority. There is no record that he made use of his position as governor to prevent the Boston church from accepting Williams's terms, but he may have hinted that he would do so if necessary, for before leaving Boston (within a few weeks), Williams expressed the dangerous opinion that civil magistrates had no authority in any religious matter, that they could not even require people to keep the Sabbath.

When Williams found that the Boston church was not pure enough for him, he made his way to Salem, where once again his charm and earnestness found an immediate response. In spite of his extreme views he never antagonized people by sanctimoniousness. He had a sweetness of spirit that clothed his harshest opinions with a mantle of holiness. He was a palpable saint, and in a society that set so high a value on sainthood, he could not fail to find men and women to follow wherever he might lead. At Salem, John Endecott, whose heart was not easily won, capitulated at once. The church made Williams the same offer that the Boston church had.

Winthrop, hearing of what had happened, was alarmed, and after conferring with the assistants wrote sharply to Endecott, "marvelling" that the Salem church would choose a teacher who held such dangerous views. Williams's charms had not yet secured a strong enough hold on Salem to withstand the disapproval of the man who had pulled the colony through the starving months just finished, and who held, besides, the authority which God gave to righteous rulers. The offer was withdrawn, and Williams departed for the Plymouth colony, where separatists were more welcome.

At Plymouth Williams was satisfied for a time. Though he worked hard at the hoe for his bread, as he later recalled, he found the church properly separated from the English churches and was content to join it and to assist the pastor by occasional preaching. William Bradford, the judicious governor of the colony, found him "a man godly and zealous, having many precious parts, but very unsettled in judgmente." Bradford was writing after the event, and his own judgment may have been unsettled by later developments, but it seems apparent that Williams's meticulous separatism proved too much even for Plymouth. In 1633, Bradford noted he "begane to fall into some strang opinions, and from opinion to practise; which caused some controversie betweene the church and him, and in the end some discontente on his parte, by occasion whereof he left them some thing abruptly."

The cause of Williams's discontent, by his own account, was the fact that the

Plymouth church had not proved as separatist as he first supposed it to be. When members of the church returned on visits to England, they attended Church of England services there, and were not cast out of the Plymouth church for doing so. In this way the Plymouth church was communicating with the churches of England and by implication acknowledging them to be true churches. Williams, by remaining a member, shared in this acknowledgement; therefore he must leave them.

According to Cotton Mather, who wrote two generations later and is not to be taken at face value, Williams was the cause of another controversy at Plymouth. He was troubled, it seems, by the application of the title "Goodman" to unregenerate persons. This term was customarily attached to the names of yeomen, who were not entitled to be called "Master" (the designation of a gentleman) but were a step above common laborers, who bore no title to their names at all. Williams contended that "Goodman" should be reserved for regenerate persons who were truly "good." This was another of those problems that zealous Puritans could become absurdly concerned about, and when Winthrop visited the colony, they put the question to him. He was able to argue away their concern, and so "put a stop to the little, idle, whimsical conceits, then beginning to grow obstreperous." Although Mather's bias is evident, the position attributed to Williams was characteristic of the man: he could follow a belief to its conclusion with a passionate literalness that bordered on the ridiculous.

When he left Plymouth, in 1633, Williams carried his zeal once more to Salem, where his memory was still green. Winthrop had remained his friend, as a letter written by Williams from Plymouth attested, but one may doubt that Winthrop was as happy as the people of Salem were to see the young man back in Massachusetts Bay. At Salem they welcomed him to church membership and cautiously made him an unofficial assistant to the pastor. By not electing him to any church office they probably thought to avoid more trouble with the government. Although the Salem church made no formal renunciation of the English churches, Williams found the members sufficiently sympathetic to his views and almost at once began to lure them along the paths of perfectionism.

While at Plymouth, Williams had raised the question whether the colonists had any right to the land they occupied. Winthrop, hearing of this, now inquired of him about it, and Williams replied with a copy of an argument he had prepared on the subject. In order to appreciate the shock which this document must have given the magistrates of Massachusetts, one must remember that the English Civil War had not begun and that the Massachusetts Bay Company had gained its control over the colony by virtue of a patent from the King. Roger Williams declared that the King's authority to grant such control rested on "a solemn public lie." He also charged the King with blasphemy for referring to Europe as Christendom and applied to the King certain uncomplimentary passages from the Book of Revelation.

The magistrates were horrified by this lese majesty and ordered Williams to appear at the next General Court to be censured. Winthrop, as shocked as the others, took steps at once to see that the confrontation between Williams and the court should not become the occasion for mutual recriminations. He wrote to Endecott, acquainting him with the summons and describing the charges which would be laid against Williams. At the same time he outlined arguments that Endecott could use in bringing Williams to reconsider and retract his offensive views: The King's claim to Massachusetts was founded on no lie, "for his people were the first, that discovered these parts: but admitt he had been mistaken: was it ever knowne, that a true Christian did give his naturall Prince the lye? was he not the Lords annointed?" This and many other arguments Winthrop adduced, some based on Scripture, some based on common sense, and some on nonsense. "If we had no right to this lande," he concluded, "yet our God hathe right to it, and if he be pleased to give it us (taking it from a people who had so longe usurped upon him, and abused his creatures) who shall controll him or his termes?"

Williams was at least sufficiently chastened to appear penitently at the court, "and gave satisfaction," Winthrop records, "of his intention and loyalty. So it was left, and nothing done in it." This was Winthrop's way of dealing with separatists, and hitherto it had worked. Perhaps even in the talented hands of Winthrop it could not have gone on working with so irrepressible a man as Williams. Perhaps the coming showdown was inevitable. But when it came, Massachusetts was in the hands of men far less able than Winthrop and fortunate indeed to have Winthrop's precedents to follow.

In November, 1634, six months after the election of Dudley, the General Court heard that Williams was publicly teaching again that the King's patent was invalid before God and that the churches of England were anti-Christian. Once again the court gave orders for his appearance. Meanwhile, Williams went on arguing with all and sundry to the effect that Massachusetts ought to send the patent back to the King, with a request that he modify it by omitting all clauses relating to donation of land. Unless this were done, the sin of accepting the land from this public liar could not be expiated except by dissolving the colony and returning all the settlers to England, where they could make public acknowledgment of the evil they had done by coming to New England on such false pretenses.

Both alternatives were ridiculous. To insult the King by telling him to rewrite the patent and leave out the lies was as fantastic as to pull up stakes and go home in order to call him a liar at closer range. When the General Court met again in March, 1635, Dudley was ready to deal with this madman, but John Cotton, in the name of the other ministers, presented a request that they be given a chance to persuade him privately of his errors. It was a reasonable request, for under Winthrop's rule they had often been consulted before the government took action on religious questions. Dudley, however, replied "that wee were deceived in him [Williams], if we thought he would condescend to learne of any of us: And what will you doe," he asked, "when you have run your course, and found all your labour lost?" Perhaps Dudley could have persuaded the Court of Assistants to let him handle Williams, but owing to his own machinations, the power of government no longer rested in the assistants alone but in the General Court of assistants and deputies. The deputies approved of the precedent set by Winthrop and, in spite of Dudley's opposition, decided to give the ministers a chance to reclaim their brother. The ministers' arguments and perhaps other "Councells from Flesh and Bloud" (as Williams later called them) induced him to abandon his attack on the charter and not to send a letter he had been preparing for the King advising His Majesty that he had been guilty of a lie.

This was the last time Williams troubled the colony about the patent, but at the next meeting of the assistants in April, 1635, he was summoned again on another score. About a year before, the magistrates had ordered that all inhabitants who were not freemen should take a resident's oath to support the colony and its government against all enemies. Roger Williams saw in this measure another source of contamination for the godly and proceeded again to sound the alarm. The difficulty lay in the fact that an oath was considered an act of worship. If a magistrate (presumably regenerate) should tender an oath to a nonfreeman (presumably unregenerate), he would "thereby have communion with a wicked man in the worship of God, and cause him to take the name of God in vain." Here was Williams's separatism cropping out in still another form. He persuaded Endecott and many others to adopt his view, and though Endecott was quickly argued out of his error, so many people were convinced the government was violating rather than upholding the word of God that the court felt obliged temporarily to drop the oath and with it the charges against Williams.

Williams's separatism now began to spin faster, and he threw off a succession of strange opinions: that a regenerate man ought not to pray in company with an unregenerate one, not even with his wife or children, and that he ought not to give thanks after the sacrament or after meals. He also resumed the dangerous contention which he had first voiced when leaving Boston in 1631, that the civil government had no authority in religious matters, that it could not punish breaches of the first table (the first four of the Ten Commandments) except in so far as such breaches caused a disturbance of civil peace.

Somehow, too, he had been able to set the people of Salem spinning with him. Indeed they were all but bewitched with his heedless holiness, and when their minister, Samuel Skelton, died, they cast off caution and in the spring of 1635 chose Williams in his place—knowing well that the government would quickly move against them.

At the next General Court in July Williams was summoned again, to answer for his growing list of erroneous opinions; and the other ministers were asked to be there too and advise the court what to do with him. As the court met, he was at the height of his furious and indefatigable righteousness and fortified by the fact that as minister of the Salem church he could now claim the acknowledged principle of congregational independence in his defense. Any attempt by other ministers to remove him from office would infringe upon the independence of the Salem church. And any attempt by the government to remove him would be met by a defiant congregation. The ministers consulted and unanimously declared their opinion that any minister who obstinately maintained such opinions as Williams avowed, "whereby a church might run into heresy, apostacy, or tyranny," should be removed, "and that the other churches ought to request the magistrates so to do." The churches might be powerless by the principle of congregational independence, but the civil government was not and prepared at once to carry out the advice of the clergy.

Salem was petitioning the General Court at this time for land in Marblehead Neck; and the General Court, ready to fight with foul means as well as fair, refused the petition unless the Salem church dismissed Williams. The outraged church immediately sent off letters to the other churches urging the members to reprimand the magistrates and the deputies alike for this "heinous sin" (which indeed it was).

In this moment of crisis the future of Williams, of Salem, and of the colony hung precariously in balance. To crush the rebellion of an entire church would have proved a difficult, if not a bloody, if not an impossible, business. To crush it in the face of any widespread sympathy would certainly have split the colony, and had the Salem appeal reached the other churches, the members might have found much in it to win their sympathy.

At this juncture the ministers evidently felt as the General Court did, that any means were justified to keep the colony and its holy commission intact. It was the ministers who received the letters addressed by Salem to the other churches, and they simply refrained from communicating them to their members. But it was Williams himself who broke the deadlock and unwittingly pulled the colony out of danger by a final extravagant gesture, a gesture which proved too much for his Salem admirers. The churches of Massachusetts, he said, had given up the principle of congregational independence and had called in the government to help suppress it. They were no longer pure churches. His congregation must therefore renounce the other churches of Massachusetts. Unless they did so, he would be obliged himself to withdraw from the Salem church.

It was unfortunate for Williams that during this crisis he was confined to his bed by an illness and so forced to resort to letters. When he could support his arguments with his winning personality, they were much more compelling than they could be in writing. Reduced to ink and paper, they were apt to appear tedious, far-fetched, sanctimonious. But even his magnetic personal charm might have been insufficient to bring the people of Salem to the step he now demanded of them. The men and women who read his letter were acutely aware that the rest of the colony was against them, that the authority of government was against them, that the wisdom of other godly ministers was against them. His letter asked them in effect to renounce all the rest of the world, for if there were no true churches in the rest of Massachusetts, where else could there be any?

Winthrop says the whole Salem church was "grieved" with Williams's request. The supreme assurance of a Roger Williams is rare at any time, and in Salem a majority were unwilling to go as far as he asked. Probably some made their decision with one eye on the land of Marblehead Neck. But it is not necessary to assume such weakness for their actions. It is more likely that the majority simply could not bring themselves to declare that everyone outside Salem was wrong.

The final confrontation between Williams and the General Court came early in October, 1635, at a full meeting, with all the ministers of the colony invited to attend. The charges preferred against him were of two kinds: his new and dangerous opinions, in particular his denial of the magistrates' authority in religious matters, and his seditious letters, one in the name of the Salem church attacking the General Court, and the second to the Salem church urging their separation from the other churches of the colony.

Williams made no attempt to deny

the charges. He was as adamant as Luther at the Diet of Worms, and though offered a month's respite in which to prepare his defense, he waived the offer and justified every opinion. Even Thomas Hooker, the most eloquent spokesman of New England orthodoxy, could not move him. The court therefore ordered him to leave the colony within six weeks.

Returning to Salem (the court was held in Boston), Williams found his church unwilling to support him. His hard core of devoted followers did not constitute a majority. Rather than remain connected with a church which recognized the other churches of Massachusetts, he resigned his office and his membership. Perhaps because he seemed thus to have drawn his own fangs, the General Court extended the date for his departure until the following spring, on condition that he not "go about to draw others to his opinions."

It was a foolish requirement. The court should have known that Williams's charm drew people like a magnet and that he was not the kind of man to be silent simply because his opinions had displeased the government. Before the winter was far gone, the magistrates heard that "he had drawn above twenty persons to his opinion, and they were intended to erect a plantation about the Narragansett Bay, from whence the infection would easily spread into these churches, (the people being, many of them, much taken with the apprehension of his godliness)." The court decided to forestall this move by shipping him back to England. But before they could lay hands on him he was gone, off for Narragansett Bay in a bitter January.

Winthrop recorded the event in his journal without comment. He held Williams's views in the utmost abhorrence, and must have concurred in the sentence of banishment. By the time the sentence was delivered there was no alternative. The people of Massachusetts could scarcely have carried out their commission and allowed Williams to remain.

That Winthrop disapproved, either openly or privately, the move to ship Williams back to England was not suggested by his journal, but it was plainly implied by Williams himself in a letter written many years later. In 1670, when Winthrop was long in his grave, Williams wrote to a friend, "When I was unkindly and unchristianly, as I believe, driven from my house and land and wife and children, (in the midst of a New England winter, now about thirty-five years past,) at Salem, that ever honored Governor, Mr. Winthrop, privately wrote to me to steer my course to Narragansett Bay and Indians, for many high and heavenly and public ends, encouraging me, from the freeness of the place from any English claims or patents. I took his prudent motion as a hint and voice from God, and waving all other thoughts and motions, I steered my course from Salem (though in winter snow, which I feel yet) unto these parts. . . ." Winthrop, unlike the other magistrates of Massachusetts, retained Williams's affection and respect. Indeed, during the first five years of his exile Williams's letters to Winthrop expressed an admiration bordering on adulation.

One of the first of these, written from Providence on October 24, 1636, answered a set of queries evidently sent by Winthrop. Now that the damage was done, Winthrop had asked his friend to cast up accounts: What had he gained by his "new-found practices"? Did he find his spirit as even as it was seven years before, when he and Winthrop first met? Was he not himself grieved to have grieved so many? Did he really think the rest of New England utterly forsaken of God? Could he not have remained in the New England churches without endangering his soul? What, after all, was he aiming at?

Williams's answers were like the man, humble and loving and respectful, but at the same time defiant, with a holy intransigeance. They breathed throughout the spirit of separatism. He did indeed think that the Lord had forsaken New England for failing to separate her churches wholly from the filthiness of English corruption. And to Winthrop he offered the very advice that Winthrop could least willingly listen to. Where Winthrop had urged him to pause and consider whether everyone was wrong but him, he replied with an invitation to join him in splendid isolation: "Abstract yourselfe," he urged, "with a holy violence from the Dung heape of this Earth." Williams would not learn the lesson which Winthrop had taught himself so painfully before he left England, that there was no escape from the dung heap of this earth; and that those who sought one or thought they had found it acted with an unholy, not a holy, violence.

Winthrop watched the subsequent development of Williams's views along a course he might have predicted. Within a year or two Williams decided that the church must not include children simply on the basis of their parents' membership and abandoned the practice of infant baptism in the congregation he had gathered among the handful of the faithful who followed him to Providence. He had himself and all the other members rebaptized, but shortly began to question whether there could be a proper church at all until God raised up some new apostolic power. Finally he reached the position where he could not conscientiously have communion with anyone but his wife.

This was the limit of his separatism. He did not reach the ultimate absurdity of finding no one but himself fit to communicate with. Indeed, from this point forward his separatism, having reached the pinnacle of isolation, broke through to a new realm of freedom, unknown and undesired by other Puritans. While still in Massachusetts he had denied that the state had anything to do with religion, thus making of it an association for purely temporal, worldly purposes. And he had espoused a congregational independence so complete that when put into practice, it necessitated a hitherto unheard of religious freedom. It must have been painful for a man who set so high a value on purity in religion to stand sponsor at Narragansett for religious opinions that he abhorred. Williams ended the pain by deciding that no church could attain purity in this world. He had effectively demonstrated the proposition to himself as he withdrew successively from the Church of England, from the churches of Massachusetts, and finally from everyone but his wife. What he saw at last was what Winthrop had tried to point out to him, that he was seeking an unattainable goal, that there was no escape from the dung heap of this earth.

Williams's reaction to this discovery was characteristic: since he could not escape the dung heap, he would embrace it. And so, Winthrop says, "having, a little before, refused communion with all, save his own wife, now he would preach to and pray with all comers."

To Winthrop this liberalism was as ridiculous as the former separatism. Williams's views on civil government had degraded the holy purpose of the state;

now he degraded the still holier purpose of the church, welcoming the mixed multitude which he had formerly complained of so bitterly in the churches of England. Many of his followers were as disgusted with his about-face as Winthrop was. It would take another fifty years before a Solomon Stoddard could demonstrate to New England that since perfect purity could not be found in the visible church, the purest course was not to seek it. To Winthrop and to other New England Puritans of the 1630's such was the counsel not of wisdom but of despair and defeat, the very thing to be expected from a man like Williams, who leaped always from one extreme to another.

Winthrop was undoubtedly pained that Massachusetts had been unable to harness the zeal of so godly a man as Williams to the cause the colony was striving for. But he could take pride in the fact that the colony had not been split apart or lured into such an irresponsible pursuit of individual holiness as Williams advocated. The great majority of the population, even the great majority of the Salem church, kept their eyes on the goal that Winthrop had set them.

It was not a goal that any man could reach by himself, but a common goal which all must seek together, with church and state working side by side. It was a goal of godliness, and it needed godly men to reach it, but not those, like Williams, who pulled too hard and left the rest behind. If such wild ones could not be tamed, it was best to cut them loose, lest they overturn the whole enterprise. Williams had proved impossible to tame. Perhaps if Winthrop, with all his conciliatory skill, had been governor, it might have been done, and Massachusetts would have been the gainer. Since it was not done, the colony was better off without so great a dissenter.

Perry Miller: Roger Williams; His Contribution to the American Tradition

Throughout his many impressive works on The Puritans, The New England Mind, Jonathan Edwards, *and more recently* Roger Williams *Perry Miller has striven to recapture the full complexity of thought with which these early Americans approached life. He has aimed to rescue them from the easy simplicities with which later admirers and critics alike had categorized them. Particularly in the case of Roger Williams he had "long been persuaded that accounts written within the last century created a figure admirable by the canons of secular liberalism, but only distantly related to the actual Williams."*

In Miller's brief biography the religious concern of Roger Williams was not a cloak for a more "fundamental" philosophy of social democracy. When Williams upheld a separation of church and state, it was not so much for the peace of the state as for the integrity of the church and of the individual religious experience. When Williams opposed the Puritan authorities of Massachusetts, it was not because he was more "modern" but because he was more Puritan than they.

IN so far as the Great Migration to Massachusetts Bay in 1630 was inspired by religion—there were of course, for many of the rank and file at least, economic inducements—it was a resolution to obey what to the leaders of this particular segment of the Puritan party seemed a clear commandment of God: to imitate the precise form of church organization described in the New Testament. These people so read the Bible as to make out what we now call a Congregational polity, which demanded two peculiar features. It declared that all churches were "particular," equal in status, and that above them there should exist no hierarchy of ecclesiastical superiors, neither bishops nor presbyteries; this equality and autonomy followed from the fact that each church was founded, at the moment of its incorporation, on an explicit and verbal covenant, publicly sworn to by the members. No one could be a churchman unless he specifically attested a concrete covenant, nor could a man be a minister apart from being so designated by a congregation; there could be no "minister at large," and hence no bishop nor presbytery. Secondly, Congregationalism required that membership be severely limited to the "visible" saints, to those openly examined before the assembled church, who could make a convincing "relation" of their spiritual experience, and who could demonstrate their ability to swear to the covenant.

On these propositions the colonizers differed not only from the established Church of England but, more disastrously, from the vast majority of their Puritan brethren, who were Presbyterians and did not believe that either the church covenant or the restricted membership was prescribed in the New Testament. The leaders of the enterprise were thus a minority within the Puritan movement; they could look ahead and see that even if the Puritans were someday to overthrow the Church of England and step into the place of the bishops, Congregational Puritans would be no better off under a Presbyterian establishment than under an Anglican.

However, save for their divergence on these peculiarities of church polity, the New Englanders had no quarrel whatsoever with the social philosophy of their day; they were entirely at one with both their Presbyterian brethren and their Anglican enemies in believing that in any society only one orthodox regime should be allowed and that the civil magistrate should suppress and, if necessary, extirpate every form of ecclesiastical or doctrinal dissent. They were legitimists, wanting to be law-abiding, conservative; they held it axiomatic that the state should protect the orthodox doctrine and way of life (once the clergy had defined it), punish heresy, and compel all inhabitants, whether church members or not, to attend services and pay taxes for the support of the ministry. They were as little capable of imagining that civil peace might comport with the allowance of religious differences as a capitalist society would be of conceiving that dissident economies may exist within the nation system.

As the sign of legitimacy, the colony had a charter, issued in 1629 by King Charles I to the Massachusetts Bay Company; this delegated royal sovereignty to the corporation, thereby empowering it to act as he did in England—to suppress heresy and put subversives to death. As a corresponding sign of legitimacy in their churches the ministers strenuously advertised that they had never separated from the Church of England. They held that church unhappily tainted by such paraphernalia as bishops and ceremonials, but said that the parish churches were Congregational at the core and therefore "true" churches. The cornerstones of the regime so rapidly and successfully established in Massachusetts were the theology of the covenant and this principle of Nonseparation. Williams was the first, and most conspicuous, to strike at these foundations. Thus he became, as indeed he remains, a menace to society.

In England these Congregational or Independent Puritans had already been acutely embarrassed by groups of the overzealous who reasoned—or rather, compulsively felt—that if a covenanted church should consist only of tried saints, then the parish churches, where everybody in a mere geographical area was regarded as a member, were hopelessly corrupt and should be denounced. They took the awful step of becoming "Separatists." (One such group, harried out of England in 1609, had, in 1620, washed up at Plymouth, where the survivors were trying to live down their past by behaving in as orthodox a fashion as their meager resources allowed.) These radicals were in no sense believers in religious liberty; they simply could not put up, even temporarily, with the established order. They were naturally regarded with horror by the authorities, but with even more loathing by the Puritans, because they justified the authorities' charge that Puritanism led to sedition, and with the utmost hatred by Congregational Puritans, because they used Congregational polity as an excuse for their rebellion. The civil and religious chiefs of the Massachusetts experiment were on the alert to detect and stamp out the slightest stirring of the Separatist spirit. Otherwise they would be convicted, in their own eyes no less than in the eyes of the world, of being an illegitimate and treasonable conspiracy, incapable of enforcing a civilized discipline.

Roger Williams was known among the fraternity in Essex to have exceptionally violent antipathies to the Book of Common Prayer and to Anglican ceremonial; it seems that there were already fears that he had embarked on the fatal descent into Separatism. These suspicions he confirmed, showing that he had indeed gone over the brink by refusing to accept the call of Boston because the people were not confessed Separatists. (That he, despite the rumors, should be offered the post shows how great was his reputation for scholarship and piety.) All his trouble at Salem from 1633 to 1635—the political heresies he there devised—were consequences of his effort to impose Separatism on Massachusetts or, failing that, to force Salem to separate from the rest of Massachusetts.

Out of this premise came his argument that the King of England had no title to the land of the Indians and so no right to issue a charter; wherefore, the colony had no warrant to enforce conformity to Nonseparation. Likewise, a people who officially believed in regenerate membership could not logically treat the unregenerate as capable of swearing to and obeying an oath; wherefore the regime had no warrant to enforce loyalty on the masses. Because he did thus threaten the very bases of the society, at a moment when the possibility of an Anglican invasion to recover the charter and to reduce Massachusetts to conformity with England was real, the state dealt with him as any state must deal with such agitators. The statesmen who exiled him never repented.

Yet now, as all the world knows, this Separatist figures in history as the pioneer of religious freedom, even of democracy. In the monumentally sculptured pantheon of international Protestantism at Geneva, where Gustavus Adolphus represents Sweden and Oliver Cromwell stands for England, the American delegate is neither Winthrop nor Cotton, but Williams. Some even hail him as the precursor of Jefferson, of liberalism and of rationalism; they call him the prophet of the splendid doctrine that a man's right to worship as he pleases is inalienably given him by nature and nature's God.

His contemporaries would be utterly bewildered by this estimate, especially those who knew why they got rid of him. To them, Williams was a recognizable—and tedious—type: one who took the Bible with a foolish literalness. The only mystery was how a scholar of his intelligence, warmth and charm could fall into this sort of pedantry, which generally flourished among boors lacking all sense of perspective. He refused to admit either his own fallibility or the practical considerations of a long-range policy; he went off half-cocked; he turned complex and subtle ideals into slapdash slogans. He was the worst kind of virtuous man, a perfectionist who made dogmas out of purity and demanded that the rest of the world conform to him rather than he to them. Roger Williams was exiled as much because he was a nuisance as because he was subversive.

It is indeed a shame that the image with which posterity has replaced the Williams whom Governor John Winthrop sent into exile bears so little relation to the fascinating reality. Winthrop, Bradford and several who opposed him felt for him an irresistible affection. A serious disservice has been done to the liberal, the Protestant, the patriotic traditions of this country by well-meaning panegyrists who, in making Williams over into their own terms, have made him unavailable to a day which has need of him. The reader of this volume will, I hope, have in his hands enough of Williams' own words to comprehend him for what he was, with all his crotchets and his magnificence, and to realize that he offers justifications for freedom which may prove more pertinent to our necessities than many of the eighteenth and nineteenth-century formulas that have tragically crumbled before our very eyes.

II

No one of those who sought his destruction—not even his archenemy, the Reverend John Cotton—would have insulted Williams by saying, as does a modern encomium: "The cast of his thought was social rather than theological." Even for theologians in an ultratheological era, the cast of Williams' mind was much too theological: therein consists his challenge to the twentieth century as well as to the seventeenth.

He came, let me repeat, to his final positions because he began as a Separatist, because he was driven by religious passion, not because he was mollified by the religious indifferentism of a Jefferson. He preached liberty of conscience not because he thought it the least destructive or most economical way for men to live together, but because of a vision which for him was a never-ending ecstasy. He did not look forward to a free society as the goal of human endeavor; instead, he looked down on it, in pity and sorrow, seeing in freedom only a preliminary requirement for the Christian pilgrimage. He remained to the end a stalwart Calvinist, believing firmly in predestination, reprobation, irresistible grace and, above all, in perseverance of the saints. Hence his rage against the Quakers. The quirk that distinguishes Williams from a Winthrop or a Cotton was simply that he took these doctrines of Calvinism with such utter consistency that rather than settle for a rough approximation to the kingdom of God on earth, he demanded the real thing or nothing at all. The cast of his mind was not social: it was so exclusively religious that to him the doctrine of the covenant as propounded in orthodox New England seemed a prostitution of theology to social expediency.

Therefore, only as a footnote to his major theme did he begin in 1631 by saying that magistrates should not enforce the duties of the "First Table"—the first four of the Ten Commandments, which pertain to the private spiritual life—and that their concern with the "Second Table" should be limited to matters like theft and adultery, which have social consequences. Winthrop and the authorities were not sympathetic, but for a while were not too much disturbed by this aberration; what worried them about Williams was his Separatism. His objections to the compulsive role of government became dangerous only after he made clear that they were linked with his effort to push Massachusetts into separation. And only after he was exiled, had suffered the snows and the hunger, only after he had learned what it meant to try to rule the explosive spirits who followed him or who trooped uninvited into his colony—only then could he think his way out of his original premise, only then recognize that what had been his minor theme had become his major. At the end of his course, he perceived that the problem for a man who wishes to guard his independence in society is how he should spiritually separate not from this or that abuse, but from society itself.

He never intended, when forbidding magistrates to enforce the First Table, to put natural right ahead of the Holy Spirit. On the contrary, he wanted to keep the state from so commanding the Christian that his endeavor for perfection would not be contaminated by social approbation. He who tries to believe as a duty of citizenship is fatally clogged. Hence, although Williams is celebrated as the prophet of religious freedom, he actually exerted little or no influence on institutional developments in America; only after the conception of liberty for all denominations had triumphed on wholly other grounds did Americans look back on Williams and invest him with his ill-fitting halo. For him there was never any virtue in freedom of and by itself; freedom was something negative, which protects men from worldly compulsions in a world where any compulsion, most of all one to virtue, increases the quantity of sin. Liberty was a way of not adding to the stock of human depravity; were men not sinful, there would be no need of freedom. When we call him a "prophet" we vulgarize the word to mean one who foretells, a prognosticator. But Williams was a prophet in the Old Testament sense, one who demands that the world listen to what the Lord Jehovah speaks through his lips. Like an Isaiah or a Jeremiah, he found himself at war with his fellow citizens because he pronounced judgment on what they thought was a good and righteous community.

So his contemporaries could recognize his disease: it was a delusion of grandeur. Where did he get the authority for his arrogance? At best he was insane; at the worst, conceited. They could not help liking him, but they wearied of his self-pity, his cloudiness, his incessant haggling over minutiae. A great many found him not so much dangerous as merely exasperating.

All this appears in the comments of those who either knew him or knew about him. Bradford was a judicious and humane man; he called Williams godly and zealous, confessing that he himself benefited from Williams' admonitions—although he insinuated that these exhortations did not always seem to agree with Scripture. Bradford held him merely unsettled in judgment, and so more to be pitied and prayed for than condemned. For years after the exile, Winthrop corresponded warmly with Williams—Winthrop's letters are lost, but Williams' replies show the tone—and broke off the interchange only when Williams showed that despite respect and affection he would fight for Rhode Island's territory against Massachusetts' aggression. Yet Williams' relations with the son of this governor, John Winthrop the younger, who for years was the foremost citizen of Connecticut and, after the charter of 1662 until his death in 1676, its governor, were those of genuine comradeship: "Your loving lines in this cold, dead season," Williams wrote him in February 1660, "were as a cup of your Connecticut cider, which we are glad to hear abounds with you, or of that western metheglin, which you and I have drunk at Bristol together"—a reference to December 1630 when the two young men had started for America together.

Thus his contemporaries saw him as a man of ability unfortunately spoiled by eccentricity. As this opinion hardened into settled conviction, we perceive that by the end of the century it had become a way of smothering his ideas. In 1680, when the battered Williams was still alive, William Hubbard composed, at the order of the General Court, a history of New England; Hubbard was a moderate and a relatively tolerant character, but he described Williams' gyrations as no more than a case of over heated zeal, remembering that even back in Essex Williams was reputed to be "divinely mad." By the time Cotton Mather wrote the *Magnalia* (published in 1702), both he and his father Increase had accepted, at least officially, the Revolution of 1689 and the Toleration Act. However, he did not on this account regard Williams as a forerunner; Williams seemed to him no apostle of liberty but simply a frenetic creature.

Mather employed a characteristically Matherian simile—it has been often quoted—of a Dutch windmill so violently turned round in a storm that the stones themselves caught fire; so, he said, was America "like to be set on fire by the rapid motion of a windmill in the head of one particular man." The trouble with Williams was psychological or even physiological: there once was a gentleman who had "an humour of making singular and fanciful expositions of Scripture," but a certain Dr. Sim gave him such a dose of "physick" as made him immediately orthodox. "Pity this Dr. Sim had but undertaken the cure of our Mr. Williams."

None of this ridicule is addressed to the Williams whom modern liberalism adores; that Williams was so little of a threat he was not worth noting. But the Williams who was divinely mad, who had a "humour," posed more of a problem for an age slowly but inexorably moving toward toleration than did the advocate of freedom. There was something in his methodology, rather than his conclusions, which aroused the real distrust, excited fear. The satires try to conceal this danger, but Mather's clumsy story of Dr. Sim betrays everything: orthodox Protestants were less alarmed by Williams' libertarianism than by the way he read the Bible. He was a maverick among the intellectuals of New England because he interpreted the relation of the Old Testament to the New not as an unfolding through time of an enduring covenant between God and man—a covenant within which men were still living and within which American governments could confidently operate—but as a radical break.

He belonged to that rare and furtive brotherhood who, here and there throughout the centuries, have taken the New Testament to mean not a continuation but a repudiation of the Old. He would be a Christian, but not a Christianized Jew. He believed the Bible from cover to cover, yet he would not read the Old Testament only as a historical document: he expounded it "typologically." Here is the secret of his Separatism and of his divergence from his colleagues (they so feared and detested it that they tried to conceal it). Here is the insight that guided him from his initial separation to his ultimate vision of the predicament of men and nations.

III

Typology is a peculiar method of interpreting the Bible, specifically the relation of the Old Testament to the New, in a way that finds inner, mystical correspondences which make unnecessary and actually irrelevant any concern for the literal, historical facts of Israel's career. The typologist, when you find him at his purest, does not care about dates nor about the social customs of Judea; he insists that events recorded in the Old Testament, including the prophecies, are preformulation of events in the life of Christ, or enunciations of principles which then were dark but the meaning of which Christ made clear. For example: Joseph descended into a pit, and Jonah into the belly of a whale; nobody can read these accounts without feeling that more is intended than the narrators comprehended, but they did not have the key and so simply told their stories. Christ solved the cryptogram: both Joseph and Jonah are "types" of His descent into hell, and Christ is the "antitype."

The chosen people enacted in history a drama they never understood, and many episodes—the drunkenness of Noah, Jacob and his concubines, the incest of Lot—would, if taken only as historical occurrences, be simply filthy. But within this dumb show was hidden a meaning; the Savior reveals to a literal-minded humanity that the Old Testament was a rehearsal to be taken not literally but figuratively. The narrative of Israel, radiating this aura of anticipation, must be translated into the doctrines of Christianity. It is not really an account of kings and harlots, but an allegory. When viewed in this light, the repressive and persecuting actions of Jewish sovereigns are not precedents for modern rulers, but typological pointers toward the methods by which, in the antitype, ministers should pronounce purely spiritual condemnations.

Typology had for centuries been a special subdivision of the allegorical method. It appears to have originated among the Alexandrine Jews in the first century of the Christian era; they, coming into contact with the sophisticated culture of Greece, were ashamed of the barbarity and crudity of their sacred books, but were relieved to discover that the Greeks long since had devised an allegorical method for extracting dignified truths out of the undignified passages of Homer. The method was introduced into Christian exegesis mainly by Origen in the third century, who found in Judaism a "veiled Christianity," and even allegorized the New Testament so that it in turn became no more than an introduction to "an unwritten and spiritual reality." From the beginning, among Jews and Christians, the allegorical method and its child, the typological interpretation, were opposed by practical men.

Typology was constantly accused of being overingenious, a subversion of the plain truths of the Gospel, of being imaginative and capricious. It was denounced as mistaking the subjectivity of overwrought brains for the firm meaning of the Bible. All this weight of Christian tradition was mobilized behind Winthrop and Cotton against what seemed to them the absurdities of Roger Williams.

The weight was especially heavy in the New England societies because these were Protestant communities; the great Protestant reformers had been very explicit in their condemnation of the typological method along with every other variant of the allegorical. Luther and Calvin depended heavily on Augustine, but primarily for support of their doctrines of predestination and divine sovereignty; they disregarded that Augustine who, in his *Confessions,* marked a stage on his road to faith when he heard "one or two places of the Old Testament resolved, and oft times in a figure [*i.e.,* in a metaphor or a type]; which when I understood literally I was slain spiritually." They pretended that Augustine had never devoted pages to proving that the drunkenness of Noah, so unedifying in the literal sense, was "a figure of the death and passion of Christ." The Reformers were the more resolved to expunge this method from Biblical exegesis because they were convinced that in the late Middle Ages (as we call them) the allegorical and typological interpretations had become a riot of irresponsible divinations.

After disciples of Bonaventura had

gone so far beyond Thomas Aquinas (who allowed, as he still today allows Thomists, the four levels of meaning—historical, moral, allegorical and analogical) as to formulate an eightfold significance, Luther thought it time to call a halt and to assert: "The literal sense of Scripture alone is the whole essence of the faith and of Christian theology." Each passage, Luther declared, has one clear, definite and true sense of its own; allegories are empty speculations, 'and as it were the scum of Holy Scripture." He called allegory and the scheme of types a "harlot" seducing "idle" men. Calvin was, if anything, more emphatic. "It is better," he said, "to confess ignorance than to play with frivolous guesses." The English Reformers, herein exhibiting perhaps their English temperament, were furiously hostile to all typological speculations. Tyndale, for example, in *The Obedience of a Christian Man,* said in 1528: "Such allegory proveth nothing, it is a mere simile. God is a Spirit, and all His words are spiritual, and His literal sense is spiritual." In the early seventeenth century, during all the bitter struggle for power between Puritans and Anglicans, both sides agreed at least on this, that a drawing of mystic meanings from the Bible was something with which men were not to be trusted.

Thus we may define Roger Williams as a man who trusted himself, trusted his reading and his insight, and was prepared to pay the price. How he came to embrace this heresy is something of a mystery, but the lines of his development are moderately clear. In most typological theory, as in Augustine's, the emphasis had been on the continuity rather than on the dislocation between the two Testaments; it endeavored to decipher a universal reign of Christian rationality by which even the most intemperate of the Jews had—unconsciously to be sure—been governed. In rage or in lust, Saul, David and Solomon had done things which, repeated within the altered framework of the risen Messiah, yielded up new instead of the hitherto baffling, not to say seductive, meanings. Typologists so strained their ingenuity to find mystical significances in Kings and Chronicles that they confirmed such forthright men as Jerome, Luther and Calvin in their conviction that the whole inquiry was both fantastic and dangerous.

Because English Puritans did read the Bible in a Protestant spirit, they found in it the description of the primitive church, and so tried to reduce the Church of England to conformity with this fact. Presbyterians, it is true, found the Apostles setting up Presbyterian churches, while the Independents interpreted them as Congregationalists; yet these differences, important as they might be, were differences of fact, not of poetic imagery.

In the same spirit, Puritan theologians —especially those who came to New England—read about the covenant which God had established with Abraham, and so organized their churches on a covenant among the saints which included their "seed." By this sort of reading, they produced a theology, an ecclesiastical program, and a social philosophy for New England. They did not entirely condemn typology; the founders of New England recognized that it, if used with extreme caution, might have its uses. John Cotton experimented with it to the very limits of safety (for that reason Williams and he were bound to become enemies), but almost to a man the New England theologians, especially such vigorous leaders as Thomas Hooker and Peter Bulkeley, were so content with the consistency of their covenant or "federal" version of the Bible that they saw in typology only a fantastic creation of the imagination which had no place in sound scholarship or in orthodox society.

Most typologists had, as I say, aimed at proving a continuity between the Testaments, at showing that a steady, unalterable scheme of law had reigned from Adam to the Apostles. But the danger always was not only that typologists might torture the Old Testament to yield up private fancies, but that, in their eagerness to make the New Testament pertain to a different order of intelligibility, they would make the division between the Testaments a chasm. If the kings of Israel were types of Christ, then they were not examples of pious conduct for modern sovereigns, and their executions of heretics and witches were no models for New England magistrates. The horror in that prospect was obvious: where then would the magistrates get any guidance to righteous political conduct?

Williams certainly formulated the logic of typology in an especially sharp, or one might even say brutal, fashion; perhaps it was because in order to become a Puritan at all he had to make the violent gesture of coming out, of separating; or possibly it was just that he had a violent imagination. At any rate, his immense distinction is that, involved with the Massachusetts oligarchy over the question of whether they should or should not declare themselves Separatists, he was forced to go farther than he had intended, and so to maintain the utter impossibility of New England's magistrates or of any other rulers or sachems in the world, being antitypes of Israel's sovereigns. The more earnestly they imitated Jewish governors, the more he was obliged to accuse them of becoming traitors to the Christian dispensation. Further meditation on the reasons which brought him to this point—in the solitude of the wilderness, amid savages and hard work—at last emboldened him to say that no modern community any longer possesses in the physical realm those sanctions with which Israel alone had been invested. Therefore the modern magistrate must get along as best he can, trying to do no more than keep the peace, while the authentic antitypes of Old Testament heroes spend their lives in this pilgrimage searching for that church which Christ destroyed and for which no earthly counterpart can any longer exist.

On this basis—and on this basis alone—Roger Williams became the prophet of religious liberty in America.

IV

Governor John Winthrop was a lawyer who thought in terms of history (his *Journal* which he kept in order to write out of it, he hoped, such a history as Bradford later achieved for Plymouth, shows how to his comprehension events fell out in seemingly illogical sequences, leaving man to find the design in the carpet, and not to cast them arbitrarily into rubrics given *a priori* by typology); as far as such a man could—or can—be, he was magnanimous. In January 1634 he wrote to John Endecott, of Salem, who hitherto had been a loyal if a somewhat impetuous soldier of orthodoxy, but who at that moment seemed seduced by the much more impetuous arguments of Williams against the charter. Winthrop had read Williams' manuscript treatise (it is lost to posterity, undoubtedly destroyed by the government), but he was not impressed. If Williams, he said, "allow not allegories, he must condemn his own writings and speeches, seeing no man useth them more than himself: and this very treatise of his exceeds all that ever I have read (of so serious an argument) in figures and flourishes."

Deep in Williams' being lay this aptitude for figures and allegories; nothing for him was more congenial, as nothing was more antipathetic to Winthrop, than to conceive of historical Israel as an allegory of a church which exists not on land or sea. Winthrop might be compared to—he was more generous than—a modern man of affairs, brought up on Longfellow, when confronted with T. S. Eliot or Kafka. As for Williams, being a rhetorician of allegory, he could not bear to see Charles I or Governor Winthrop take unto themselves those accouterments of power which Christ had turned into metaphors.

Winthrop was a modest man, but he saw in himself another Joshua: he asked Endecott to compare the one history with the other. Even Williams would have to admit that before the settlement of Massachusetts, God Himself had wiped out the Indians by a plague; this was not a fact to be ignored according to the scheme of cause and effect which constitutes history rather than poetry. Was it not within the same dimension of divine providence as were similar interventions in the Old Testament? "If we had no right to this land, yet our God hath right to it, and if He be pleased to give it us (taking it from a people who had so long usurped upon him, and abused His creatures), who shall control Him or His terms?" If you have to deal with the concrete facts of America just as they come up, one by one, and thereafter a providential design appears among them leading to success, why should this pattern be condemned simply because it happens to resemble the sort of favor shown by the same Jehovah to the chosen people of old? Why condemn it in the name of some other standard, some fanciful construct of an allegory? Why hesitate to regard yourself as chosen?

In 1636 Winthrop was consoled to receive from a reliable English correspondent, who had known Williams before 1630, an assurance that Williams was "passionate and precipitate." He was even more reassured in 1637, in the midst of the agony of the Anne Hutchinson crisis, to hear from an anonymous friend an account of the gossip in Puritan circles accusing New England of Separatism, which complimented him to this extent: "Your disclaiming of Mr. Williams' opinions and your dealing with him so as we hear you did, took off much prejudice from you with us, and hath stopped the mouths of some." Winthrop was cautious—after all, who could tell, there might be something in this allegorizing—but in May 1637, when he defended an order of the General Court permitting the authorities to expel undesirables (that is, those whom the magistrates thought sympathetic to Anne Hutchinson), oddly enough he struck not at Anne's Antinomians but at his friend Williams:

> Admit a true Christian should come over, and should maintain community of goods, or that magistrates ought not to punish the breakers of the First Table or the members of churches for criminal offences, or that no man were bound to be subject to those laws or magistrates to which they should not give an explicit consent: I hope no man will say that not to receive such a one were to reject Christ. For such opinions (though being maintained in simple ignorance, they might stand with a state of grace, yet) they may be so dangerous to the public weal in many respects, as it would be our sin and unfaithful-

ness to receive such among us, except it were for trial of their reformation.

Williams might dazzle him with ingenious readings of the Bible, but a hard-pressed executive like Winthrop knew what could be tolerated and what could not in a society for which he was responsible.

Meanwhile he was getting reports from the exile about Indian maneuvers in the Pequot country, which were superb pieces of military intelligence. But along with them came more and more weird preachments. The Pequots may have committed murder, but still they were not comparable to the servants who slew King Joash, for he was a "type of Jesus." Just how the head of a state at war was to distinguish between ordinary murderers and those who had slain a type of Jesus remained obscure to John Winthrop. He was hardly enlightened in July 1637, when he received a thirty-seven page treatise from Providence (it too has perished) on "the differences between Israel and all other states." But he could hardly miss the point of the admonition accompanying the discourse, and certainly could not be expected, when thus addressed, to accept the consequences of such a distinction between type and antitype:

> I know, and am persuaded that your misguidings are great and lamentable, and the further you pass in your way, the further you wander, and have the further to come back; and the end of one vexation will be but the beginning of another, till conscience be permitted (though erroneous) to be free amongst you.

We may indeed feel that Winthrop was tried beyond the limits of charity, when, just as victory was being won and the heathen were being either slaughtered or taken in gratifying numbers—exactly as enemies of the Israelites fared in the Old Testament—he should receive a plea from Williams for mercy toward the captives: "Sir, concerning captives (pardon my wonted boldness), the Scripture is full of mystery, and the Old Testament of types."

Clearly the man had gone mad, like all megalomaniacs, meditating on only one subject. The wisdom of sober Christianity, especially of Protestantism, had always warned that in typology such madness lay. This typologist justified suspicion by coming up, out of all his hardship, with a blanket pronouncement that even erroneous consciences should be tolerated in civilized society and savage prisoners ought to be set free!

V

Only a few letters survive out of Williams' writings during the years of his controversy with Massachusetts (although, as we have seen, he wrote at least two tracts): so we have to make out his development from guarded entries in Winthrop's *Journal*, or from Williams' later and highly colored reminiscences. But the best evidences of what happened to his mind are the great publications of 1644.

He reached Boston in 1631 persuaded that truly reformed churches ought to separate and magistrates should not spoil the first four Commandments by enforcing them. That he should hold these positions out of nothing more than a too-eager Puritanism was comprehensible to those who disagreed with him, who had dealt with similar extremists (as they had dealt with John Endecott) and brought them back to sanity. But instead of yielding to the logic of Winthrop and of demonstrable history—instead of seeing what clearly was to be seen by the most recent arrival in America: that this state was a covenanted people and therefore a reproduction in the wilderness of sanctified Israel—Williams alone among the settlers persisted in saying that such patriotism was based on a misreading of the Bible. (Anne Hutchinson and her Antinomians never came anywhere near this idea.) Why Williams thus stood out may be translated, though at great risk, into some such modern equivalent as a principle of literary criticism.

The deeper he progressed into the structure of allegory and metaphor, the more he found the Old Testament a prophetic rather than a factual book. But the more he understood that it was not to be taken literally, the more he estranged himself from the historical mentality that proposed to govern Massachusetts and Connecticut in Israel's image. The orthodox accused him of an inability to read the Bible in the light of circumstances and conditions—they said he imposed on it meanings invented by himself; he became thereby the more convinced that they, in an eagerness to accommodate allegory to their self-interest, had lost the meaning of Christianity.

By the time the score was added up, and Williams had endured the winter of flight—by the time he had become the indispensable intermediary between his antagonists and the heathen fury—he found out why he had first preached Separatism: the nation of Israel had never, in historical fact, been such a model of charity as Winthrop expected to create in America. It had never been anything more than a type, imperfect and physical, of an ideal which was as unattainable in America as in Europe. Wherefore, governments which, like that of Massachusetts, pretended to follow the example of Israel, were behind the times. (Williams might have said, but did not, that it was as though a prince should try to imitate Hamlet, not realizing that *Hamlet* is a literary creation.) Persecution of dissidents, in communities possessing no other guidance than the calculus of sinful nature, was no way to become the antitype. A break had occurred in history; the model was no model; only the sword of the spirit should any longer have real effect. Mere governments had better allow as much freedom as possible. . . .

In the summer of 1636, in his refuge at Providence—having survived the terrible winter with the help of only God and a few stray Indians—Roger Williams had in his hands three documents that humiliated and outraged him.

First, he had a manuscript which John Cotton had written during the winter (either when Williams was in the thick of his fight at Salem or else when he was shivering in the wilderness), the "Answer" to four chapters in a book presented to him for comment by one John Hall, of Roxbury. *A Most Humble Supplication of the King's Majesty's Loyal Subjects* was printed (no doubt surreptitiously) in 1620, purporting to be written by an Anabaptist imprisoned, as he said, "for his conscience," in Newgate. Deprived of ink, he penned his thoughts with milk and smuggled out the pages to his fellows. Cotton newly installed in the foremost position in the colony—teacher of the Church of Boston—pontifically replied in accents revealing that he already assumed himself to be dean of the colonial clergy; his reply did not quite satisfy Hall (who later moved to

Connecticut), and so Hall sent the manuscript to Williams, who had time to ponder it.

The second document was a treatise of eleven "heads," each buttressed with copied quotation from Scripture, sent by the associated ministers of Massachusetts Bay to the people of Salem in the autumn of 1635. Williams had not seen it in Salem, but he knew it had been effective in persuading a majority of the congregation to turn against him. Entitled *A Model of Church and Civil Power,* it was a concise summary of the position Massachusetts had arrived at in the philosophy of church and state, after having by the act of migration completed its revolution and stabilized itself on the basis of a Nonseparatist orthodoxy. Cotton, we know, had nothing to do with writing it but Williams believed that he did. Williams wanted to see it, and in the summer Elder Sharpe sent him a copy from Salem.

The third document was by far the most galling: it was a haughty letter written directly to Williams by John Cotton himself, in this same summer, telling him why he was banished, exulting in the sentence, and calling on him to repent. It was a calculated insult, striking a man who was down and all but out.

What the three added up to showed, or seemed to show, that not only was John Cotton the most implacable of Williams' foes but that he was the mainspring of a malignant conspiracy in Boston which would not rest until they had destroyed him. There were many reasons why between these two the struggle should be unto the death. In the first place, back in Essex before the migration Williams had dared rebuke the great and much-esteemed Cotton for complying with the Book of Common Prayer. Secondly, Cotton now occupied the throne in Boston which could have been Williams' had Williams not refused it out of a scruple of conscience; where Cotton now lorded it, Williams could have strutted had he been able to swallow the casuistry of Nonseparation.

Furthermore, there is the still deeper reason: Cotton had shown himself in theology the least legalistic, the most responsive to allegories and typologies, of all theologians who came to New England. Williams would know better than to suppose that down-to-earth federalists like Thomas Hooker would have anything but contempt for his inspired readings of the Bible, but something more might be expected of Cotton, on whom Hooker had long looked askance. Like Mrs. Hutchinson, Williams expected Cotton to live up to the vision he imparted to his followers. Cotton failed Williams, as the next year he also failed Anne Hutchinson; henceforth the very existence of these two was for him a standing rebuke. Williams' grief over what he considered this betrayal was profound, but Cotton's hatred became a family heirloom, to be passed on to his sons and grandsons.

But still the deepest of all reasons for this hostility was the fact that Cotton, so widely renowned among Puritans in England and Calvinists on the Continent, became the symbol of the New England Way. More than any other he assured the world that a Congregational system could get along with, indeed required, a vigorous magistracy, that churches founded on an exclusive covenant and consisting only of tried saints were entirely compatible with a forcible and intolerant rule of uniformity. He was the incarnation of that image of respectability, conformity, success (all the more because he was supposed in his youth to have been radical and to have suffered for nonconformity), which has since dominated American spiritual and intellectual life. Williams is the first in our history to rebel against this examplar, to prefer going into the wilderness out of devotion to an idea which men like Cotton could grandly explain was altogether crack-brained and not to be taken seriously. . . .

From the beginning to the end, Williams was always in his theological creed an orthodox Calvinist; the six fundamentals he recited to Cotton remained truly fundamental, and the authority of the Bible was absolute. The only heresy that separated him from Cotton and the orthodox was his typology, but once he substituted that different premise, he reasoned very much as they did. Like them, or even more than were they, he was a "strict constructionist" of Scripture. He wanted the state to enforce the same moral regulations that were on the statute books of Massachusetts; but he could not see how a government in the modern dispensation, without the sanctions given to a type, could achieve such efficiency in administration as was Israel's by divine appointment: "Adultery," he wrote the young Winthrop, "is a fire which will root out, but the gentiles, the nations of the world, will never be proved capable of such laws and punishments as that holy nation, bred up and fed with miraculous dispensations, were fit for." So in the 1670's Williams was caught in a stick he himself had cleft when the Quakers, availing themselves of Rhode Island's freedom, poured in, not only disturbing the civil peace but preaching a theology which shocked Williams as profoundly as his typology had scandalized John Cotton.

Modern admirers who try to fit Williams into their pattern of liberality regard his opposition to the Quakers as a blot on his record, as a failing of senility. Thus they betray an utter failure to comprehend Williams' mind. We need to remind ourselves that the Quakers who, in those first intoxicating days, followed George Fox and Edward Burrough were not the sober citizenry of today but a mob of crassly assertive, ignorant and reckless fanatics. They preached an absolute authority of the inner light, of a direct inward communication from on high, which to a Biblicist like Williams —for whom the personal Jesus, crucified in Jerusalem, was the central and decisive fact in history—seemed an even more disastrous subordination of revelation to mere man-made fantasy than the political covenant taught in Boston. In his lame old age, Williams fought the Quakers for the same reason that he had fought Cotton in his manhood: any hasty generalization, arrived at without fear and trembling, without punctilious respect for the Word—whether it be a wrong interpretation of the covenant or the prompting of an impulse called the inward light—crystallizes into self-righteousness. Once the typological insight is granted, the Bible becomes an instrument for the shattering of self-esteem—wherefore Williams was not, nor could he ever have become, a liberal in the Jeffersonian or Utilitarian sense.

There was, on the other hand, nothing of the mystic or pantheist about him: the Bible was law, the physical universe was divinely governed but not infused with divinity. He was simply aghast that Fox should speak of saints as indissolubly united with the essence of

God, for "the essence of being of the immortal, invisible, infinite, eternal, omnipotent and omniscient, and wise, we know no more than a fly knows what a king is." To him, this sort of self-infatuation was bound to become what later generations call solipsism. He was, at heart, so much the Puritan that he demanded first of all a respect for the objective reality of the created universe (even though it be a vale of tears), and distrusted with every fiber of his being a theology of influx which was certain to deny the tangibility of existence.

> Let this proud Fox, or any of the stoutest lions or lionesses amongst them, look but a few minutes upon the glorious sun in the heavens, and then tell us how their eyes do: and yet thus like proud and prattling children do they make a noise about their bibs and aprons and muckingers, and how they are one with God in His being and essence.

The all-important distinction between creation and immanence comes out, for instance, in such a cry as this:

> It is not enough for sun, moon, and stars, and men to be enlightened by His infinity, but they must be God Himself, and light itself, in the sense, because God is light.

Thus it seemed to Williams—here I think the modern spirit should heed him—that whoever speaks with the accents of spiritual finality, whether an Endecott or a Fox (even though Fox renounces the use of force), is a danger to the spirit. Williams' greatest insight is into the corrosive effects not of sin but of virtue. The worst enemy of the soul is not the profane antagonist or persecutor, but the soul's rectitude. Every gathering of the righteous into a society of purity, in which the Bible becomes only a support to the aims of the community, is a fatal temptation. The Quakers seemed the most insidious form of this temptation yet let loose on a susceptible people. . . .

EPILOGUE: THE SIGNIFICANCE OF ROGER WILLIAMS FOR THE AMERICAN TRADITION

For the subsequent history of what became the United States, Roger Williams possesses one indubitable importance, that he stands at the beginning of it. Just as some great experience in the youth of a person is ever afterward a determinant of his personality, so the American character has inevitably been molded by the fact that in the first years of colonization there arose this prophet of religious liberty. Later generations may not always have understood his thought; they may have imagined that his premises were something other than the actual ones, but they could not forget him or deny him. He exerted little or no direct influence on theorists of the Revolution and the Constitution, who drew on quite different intellectual sources, yet as a figure and a reputation he was always there to remind Americans that no other conclusion than absolute religious freedom was feasible in this society. The image of him in conflict with the righteous founders of New England could not be obliterated; all later righteous men would be tormented by it until they learned to accept his basic thesis, that virtue gives them no right to impose on others their own definitions. As a symbol, Williams has become an integral element in the meaning of American democracy along with Jefferson and Lincoln.

However, the student of Williams' own writings will, I trust, perceive that great as has been his symbolic role, he himself was thinking on a deeper plane than that which simply recognizes religious liberty as a way for men to live peaceably together. He was not a rationalist and a utilitarian who gave up the effort to maintain an orthodoxy because he had no real concern about religious truth, but was the most passionately religious of men. Hence he is an analyst, an explorer into the dark places, of the very nature of freedom. His decision to leave denominations free to worship as they chose came as a consequence of his insight that freedom is a condition of the spirit.

Of course, as these selections show, this statement needs to be qualified by the observation that Williams was the devotee of a method of Biblical interpretation which most modern intelligences reject. Hence he came to the problem of freedom not as a disinterested philosopher but as a doctrinaire exponent of a peculiar and highly suspect version of Scripture. Theologically he was an orthodox Calvinist, and like all Calvinists can be accused of Bibliolatry. No one aware of archaeology, textual criticism, historical research, or comparative religion can today so naïvely maintain that the Old Testament is a collection of types of which the New is the antitype, or so rashly look on all nature itself as a typological preaching of Christianity.

Hence the endeavor to understand Williams requires some grasp of his notions of exegesis; if the only reward of such an investigation were to be a familiarity with the typological method, the effort would hardly be worth the making by any except antiquarians. Yet for us the real meaning of Williams' thought is not the content of his typology but what, through the practice of it, he came to demand from society. This was nothing less than that it respect sincerely-held opinions, no matter how bizarre they might seem to the authorities. Out of the exercise of his imagination he perceived that no man can be so sure of any formulation of eternal truth as to have a right to impose on the mind and spirit of other men. Williams further realized that he who does so impose truth on others is no longer concerned, in his heart of hearts, with the truth but only with the imposition. That the social order has to be maintained, that civil peace must be enforced and the laws obeyed, he made clear in the letter of 1655. But what he stood for, and still stands for, is the certainty that those who mistake their own assurances for divinely appointed missions, and so far forget the sanctity of others' persuasion as to try reducing them to conformity by physical means, commit in the face of the Divine a sin more outrageous than any of the statutory crimes.

Or to put it in other words, Roger Williams was a profound Christian who, like Pascal, refused to identify the Christian vision with worldly appearances, with either any political order or even the words of the Bible itself. He knew that the meaning of life lies not on the surface, but somewhere underneath, and that it must be perpetually sought. He attacked the political pedant and the textual literalist, not because they are evil men or their motives not admirable, but because they do not recognize the true nature of freedom. They lose the essential in the circumstantial, and so deceive themselves into making of their virtue an instrument of tyranny. They destroy not the liberty of others but their own.

Hence, in order that men might be protected against the folly of their virtues, Williams insisted on the need for law and order, and at the same time on the utmost allowance within the broad confines of civil peace for every shade of opinion, even the most foolish. By exposing false conceptions of purity and loyalty, he opened the way for a self-distrusting, undogmatic and yet firm resolution to seek for those goals in which alone the soul of man finds fulfillment. So indeed he does remain the symbolic embodiment of that heroism which resists all those who, under whatever slogan, would force the conscience to things it cannot abide. Having bought truth dear, as he says in the best of this prose, we must not sell it cheap, not even for what seems to be the saving of our souls, least of all for the sake of worldly reputation. Wherefore, he was able to contend through a long life for the essential freedom, saying constantly that if he perished, he perished, that eternity would pay for all. In the end, it may be that he is most valuable to us because he incarnates the fighter for ends who keeps always present to his consciousness a sense of his own fallibility, of his own insignificance, without ever for that reason giving over, without ever relaxing, the effort.

Alan Simpson: SALVATION THROUGH SEPARATION

A chapter from Alan Simpson's study of Puritanism in Old and New England *provides an important final perspective in assessing the significance of Roger Williams's conflict with the Massachusetts authorities. Simpson stressed again that the source of Williams's thought lay in his concern for a purer religion rather than a purer democracy, that in nine-tenths of his opinions "Williams saw eye to eye with the Cottons and Winthrops who banished him," and that religious liberty appeared to Williams even more necessary for the health of the church than for the peace of the state. Simpson's particular contribution was to explain more clearly than previous historians how the positions both of Williams and of the Massachusetts authorities fitted into the full context of the Puritan movement on both sides of the Atlantic. Finally, for those inclined to see a guarantee of religious vitality in the separation of church and state, Simpson described how worldly pressures came to obscure the religious spirit amid the liberty of Rhode Island as well as within the conformity of Massachusetts.*

IT is the thesis of this book that Puritans were elect spirits, segregated from the mass of mankind by an experience of conversion, fired by the sense that God was using them to revolutionize human history, and committed to the execution of his Will. As such, they formed a crusading force of immense energy; but it was an energy which was incapable of united action, as the elect souls formed very different conceptions of what the Divine Will entailed for themselves, their churches, and the unregenerate world outside the circle of the saved. It was also an energy which everywhere subsided from an ecstasy of zeal into standardized patterns of behavior, as successive waves of enthusiasm were broken on the resistant forces of human nature and as men who had dreamed of a holy community found themselves simply the administrators of a Puritan tradition.

In my last chapter I dealt with one attempt to create a framework of institutions within which the regeneration of fallen man—that miracle of rebirth within the human soul which formed the grand object of all Puritan striving—might go on indefinitely. That attempt was the covenanted community erected in the wilderness by the founders of Plymouth, Massachusetts, New Haven, and Connecticut. In the covenanted community the basic principle was the conviction that the elect soul perceives in Scripture a form of worship appointed by God for man which church and state must sustain. All problems of conscience are resolved by a spiritual aristocracy, which applies its regenerate reason to the Word of God and enforces its findings on the community. Conversions, upon which the aristocracy depends for its renewal, though theoretically a matter of God's arbitrary pleasure, are expected to occur within the means offered by the church. The converted, if they are rightly instructed, will not challenge the orthodoxy which the church upholds. If they persist in erroneous opinions, the church will marshal its resources of grace and learning to produce repentance. If they do not repent, they will be proceeded against as blasphemers, idolators, schismatics, or heretics in accordance with the schedule of ecclesiastical errors. The state, which is simply the police department of the church, stands by to deal with them with the powers of punishment which can be brought to bear on the outward man: flogging, imprisonment, banishment, or execution. As for the unregenerate—that is to say, the majority of mankind who can obviously make no kind of claim to a work of grace in their souls—they will be protected in such civil rights as God intended them to have, exposed to the sermons which will save a few of them, and prevented from dishonoring the community by scandalous conduct.

This interpretation of the obligations and privileges of the covenant between God and the elect soul was general throughout the Right and Center of the Puritan movement as Puritans passed from opposition into power. Though repellent to us, it ought to be appreciated in the context of a century-old tradition in which the societies of western Europe acknowledged a dogmatic commitment to the truths of Christianity. Working within that tradition, the first impulse of the Puritan saint was to erect a theocracy. But to attempt to do so was to try to seal off all the explosive possibilities of the conversion experience, and those who did so, either in New England or in Old England, found themselves confronted by a series of rebellions from saints who refused to be confined within the new orthodoxies. It is the purpose of this chapter to examine the extreme form which these rebellions assumed: the discovery that the saints' mission is to separate the church from the state. I shall first consider, in general terms, how the saints were led to this decision and what problems it created for them. I shall then examine Rhode Island as an attempt to fulfil the Puritan mission within the forms of religious freedom.

How does the Puritan saint convince himself that he must dissolve the church of tradition into a voluntary association and deny to the state any coercive power or positive duty in relation to religion? The development is complex; there are many different routes and many different degrees of separation. An early tendency in this direction is seen whenever the saint discovers that the church cannot be made to come up to his standards. The perfection that he seeks can be achieved only through withdrawal. The gulf that separates the regenerate soul from the natural man becomes absolute in his eyes, and any attempt to bridge it is a corruption. So, asserting the privileges of his new birth and aspiring to the purity which is only imaginable in a sect, he claims his liberty from both ecclesiastical and civil authority.

This impulse may have one of three results. First, it may carry him, as it carried the Anabaptists, into a complete repudiation of society and a search for absolute segregation within the crevices or on the frontiers of civilized life. Second, it may be arrested and stabilized in a theory of religious liberty: the saint proposes to live in society and to obey its laws, but he demands absolute freedom of worship. In the third contingency, the separatist becomes a militant millenarian, only withdrawing from the world in order to come back again with a sword in his hand. Both extremes—the retreat into a fortress for the pure and the militant return—had been vividly demonstrated when the mysteries of regeneration were first explored in Luther's day, and the prospects of a middle way were often to hang precariously balanced between the two.

A later tendency which reinforced these prospects, in certain situations, was the discovery that, as saints differed so much, no saint was likely to enjoy any liberty for his own conscience unless he was prepared to guarantee liberty to others. One is reminded of Voltaire's pleasantry: "If there had been in England only one religion, its despotism would have been fearful. If there had been two religions, they would have cut each other's throat. But as there are thirty, they live peacefully and happily." This perception of the need for toleration in a divided Christendom was often a reluctant discovery, but an agreement to live and let live was bound to impose itself on some minds as a practical necessity, and it could become a matter of principle on the assumption that God had still much to reveal and that his preferred method of revealing it was through the free competition of prophecy. However, though all separatists used these arguments, not all who used them became separatists. They were arguments for varying degrees of toleration, and more was needed than this to turn a tolerationist into the kind of man who would insist that in religious belief the individual conscience was alone binding.

When one turns to the famous names among the separatists thrown up by English Puritanism—Williams, Milton, Vane, Saltmarsh, Dell, the Quakers—generalization is still difficult, as each structures his opinions with the terms of his own piety. What is clear is that all have passed through an intense religious experience; that all recoil from the external discipline which orthodox Puritanism tries to insert between the regenerate conscience and God; that all combine an acute sense of the uncertainty of human judgment in the past with an abounding confidence in the revelation that is going on around them; and that most of them are either pronounced rationalists or pronounced mystics. These two paths, rationalism and mysticism, are not the only routes, but they are among the more obvious. If the regenerate soul fastens on rationality as the essence of God's revealed will, and on reason as the faculty through which man, made in the image of God, is to relate himself to his maker and his fellow-men, he is liable to discover that the regenerate life is a life of free inquiry and free moral choice and to spend his whole pilgrimage trying to substitute self determination for submission to any outward law. This is what Christian liberty came to mean for Milton. It is a doctrine of conscience which embraces the idea of the individual as a church in himself and employs every resource of prophetic scorn against the notion that ecclesiastical or civil coercion can contribute anything to the growth of grace. Alternatively, the mystic, envisaging God as spirit and believing himself possessed by it, transcending all the means offered by the church in his mystic union, and protesting in both his noble and his lunatic moods the sovereign right of the spirit to free expression in this glorious age of testimony—who was more likely to reach the conclusion that church and state must be separated? A secure church can either contain its mystics or dismiss them into heresy. A church shattered by a chain reaction of spiritual energy invites replacement by mystics who claim for themselves exactly the same authority as the apostles. Such were the Quakers, and Quakerism was simply the end result of tendencies which are clearly seen in Vane, Saltmarsh, and Dell and which had led them to insist on separatism.

So much for the experience which is liable to turn a saint into a separatist: one, that is to say, who will demand complete freedom for the religious conscience from ecclesiastical or civil authority and who is willing to forego any claim by the godly to govern society.

What were his problems? His first problem was to convince everyone outside his own fraternity that he had a right to start his experiment. He was flouting the tradition of a thousand years, and everything about him seemed an outrage to right-minded people. Perhaps a start could be made on the frontier. But in England the experiment could be made only through revolution and military dictatorship. In that event two things happened. All separatists, except the Quakers, abandoned one half of their profession in order to enjoy the half which mattered more. They became theocrats in spite of themselves, because the liberty which they demanded for the religious conscience—the freedom to worship, to prophesy, and to dismantle, if they could, every remnant of an established church—could be enjoyed only if saints like themselves wielded a dictatorial power over the political community. At this point freedom for the regenerate has come to mean, once again, the coercion of the natural man: the kind of coercion which Cromwell practiced when he governed through military despotism, or which Vane and Milton were driven into. The other possibility has already been touched on. In the wild excitements of revolution many of the separatists became militant millenarians under the impression that the hour had struck for the saints to inherit the earth.

The second problem, assuming that the experiment could be begun without a revolution, was to demonstrate that the emancipated conscience was capable of submitting to any social discipline. Its critics were convinced it could not. It seemed to them, not without reason, to be the kind of anarchism which dissolved all obligations, and especially the obligation of the lower classes to stay in their places. It remained to be seen whether it would work on the frontier.

The third problem, if the other two were successfully solved, was to see if the Puritan impulse could conserve itself any better within the forms of religious freedom than elsewhere.

The colony of Rhode Island was not planned by anybody. It scratched and clambered into existence out of bands of fugitives and exiles who were either ejected out of Massachusetts or chose to try their fortune elsewhere. Its settlers included prophets and prophetesses; inspired tanners, tailors, and tapsters; disgruntled elders; characters like Captain Underhill, who enjoyed saying that after years of useless churchgoing he had found himself saved while smoking a pipe of tobacco; soldiers of fortune; and a lot of little people whose only object in life was to get themselves a bit of land and see how many other bits they could add to it. However, of the six personalities who dominated this little theater in the wilderness, four of them—Roger Williams, Anne Hutchinson, John Clark, and Samuel Gorton—were definitely prophets; a fifth, William Coddington, began his exile with a mosaic flourish; and the sixth, William Harris, found it entirely natural to enliven his real estate operations with an appeal to the sovereign rights of conscience.

To see the separatist thrust at work in some of these prophets, let me pause a moment over two of them: Roger Williams and Samuel Gorton.

In nine-tenths of his opinions Roger Williams saw eye to eye with the Cottons and Winthrops who banished him. Like them, he thought that salvation was all that mattered, believed in predestination, preached the new birth and the life of rigorous self-examination and self-denial that followed. The little treatise which he wrote for his wife's guidance, called *Experiments of Spiritual Life and Health,* and the steadfast resistance which he put up during his impetuous pilgrimage to all the seductions of "honor, profit, and preferment" which beguile the unwary in this world would both command their approval. Like them, he treated Scripture as an absolute authority and used the same tools of learned analysis to expound it. Nor did he break with them because he had any quarrel with aristocracy as a principle of political government or any ambition to found a democratic community. He broke with them because he convinced himself, in a series of collisions with the Massachusetts authorities, that they were not taking sufficiently seriously the gulf which separates the regenerate from the unregenerate and that the covenanted community of the New England pattern was actually a horrible perversion of God's declared Will.

Williams' arguments, as they were developed in the course of a long controversy with orthodoxies in both New and Old England, are notoriously difficult to summarize. The main features, as they appear and reappear through the churnings of biblical polemic, are threefold. First, an exposition of New Testament texts, such as the parable of the wheat and the tares, to demonstrate that the most erroneous conscience imaginable is not to be disturbed in its errors by force; second, a ruthless disposal of all the Old Testament precedents by the device of "typology," which I shall explain shortly; and, third, a series of scattered but razor-sharp expositions of the nature of church and state as utterly different societies. But all this is imbedded in very wearisome prose, and it is made more complicated by the fact that he has absorbed many other arguments which his predecessors had struck off in the past century. Personally, I find him easiest to understand when I fasten on three positions which he offered to defend in public debate toward the end of his stormy career. First, that forced worship stinks in God's nostrils; second, that forced worship denies the coming of Christ by insisting on the national church of the Jews; third, that religious liberty is the only prudent, Christian way of preserving peace in the world.

When Williams reflects on the history of the effort to enforce religious orthodoxy, two impressions seem to occur to him: such efforts misunderstand the church (that is to say, they are incompatible with the nature of those who profess to be elected) and they destroy the civil peace which God has commanded for both the elect and the natural man during their earthly pilgrimage. To the degree that the welfare of the church transcends the welfare of natural man, the first consideration has the priority. The real sufferers from the doctrine of forced worship have always been the saints. It places them at the mercy of any error which clerical authority may commit, as Williams himself had been victimized by the Massachusetts hierarchy. It invites the natural man, through his representative, the political government, to impose his ideas in a realm in which he is absolutely unfit to have an opinion. It fosters the delusion that the "garden of the church"—that hedged inclosure for a few rare blooms—was ever intended to embrace "the wilderness of the world." It obscures the true nature of conscience as a faculty which is bound to judge differently until the day when God chooses to enlighten it fully. The only escape from these monstrosities is to realize that regeneration is a spiritual process, to be promoted by purely spiritual means, including the unimpeded testimony of prophets through whom the spirit is speaking to this age.

But if forced worship stinks in God's nostrils, how is this to be reconciled with the first four of the Ten Commandments? Has the Gospel destroyed the Law? New England had built its orthodoxy on those commandments. Puritans in Old England who discovered reasons for toleration had great difficulty in believing that a Christian magistrate had no duty under those commandments to repress false worship. Ireton was to speak for them on one occasion when he checked the appeal to Christ's ministry with the obvious retort: "It is not enough to show us what Christ preached: it is necessary to show us how the duty given to the magistrate under the Old Testament has been superseded under the New." Williams got rid of this difficulty by a sweeping use of the device of typology which was frequently employed to relate the Old Testament to the New, but seldom as boldly as this. The construction placed upon these commandments by the Jews was not to be taken as a literal model by John Cotton or anybody else. It was to be understood as a symbol of the spiritual church of Christ, and to invoke it as a model for coercive institutions was in effect to deny the coming of Christ.

So forced worship stinks because it is perverting God's plan for the regeneration of souls. But it is also frustrating his command that the regenerate man and the natural man must live together in peace. The saint is not "of the world," but he must live in it, under a temporal regime of law which protects the civil rights of both the saved and the damned. But what security can mankind enjoy for their bodies and goods, what peace is possible during these centuries of religious warfare, so long as the world is trapped in the fallacies of forced worship? The agency for providing this security is the state, and the natural reason given by God to all mankind is the only guaranty we possess. Doubtless it is insufficient to prevent sin from committing its enormities, but it has sufficed to produce long periods of peace where the name of Christ was never heard of, and it will be made less, not more, sufficient by intruding the claims of the saints in a sphere where they do not belong. If they cannot advance Christ's kingdom by claiming earthly power, neither can they promote the peace of the world. God gave his saints no commission to rule the world, as we might guess, if no other reasons existed, from the fact that he chooses them from ranks which are rich in faith but poor in worldly skill. So little have they in common with the men who have governed the world throughout its history! Yet, damned as the ruling classes almost certainly are, in Williams' estimate, it is still their business to rule.

It was in this spirit that Williams was prepared to generalize his case for what he called "soul liberty." Taken literally, it meant that the church would simply be a voluntary corporation within a secularized state and that churches, true and false, would have the same liberty. As such, it was one of the most breathtaking demands ever made.

Samuel Gorton, though a rich and redoubtable figure, need not detain us so long. Massachusetts, with that weakness for attributing gratuitous sins to its enemies, which was always a Puritan failing, was to accuse him of having run away from England to escape a debt. But there is no reason to doubt his own word that he came to enjoy the privileges of election, among them the privilege of prophecy. He arrived, however, in the midst of the Antinomian controversy, when prophets of his own stamp, like Anne Hutchinson, were being weeded out, so either for that reason or for some other he withdrew to Plymouth. There, however, after the first good impression which a godly man was bound to make, there began to be grave doubts about what they had welcomed. The new inhabitant, to use his favorite description of himself, was "a professor of the mysteries of Christ," with his own access to divine knowledge and alarming talents for conversion—talents so alarming that several citizens who had enjoyed the benefits of his parlor prophecies, including a minister's wife, began to make very unflattering comparisons between the official religion and the professor's. And so began the first of many brawls in which the professor, after giving a fine display of Divine knowledge, legal knowledge, and demagoguery, was naturally banished. From his point of view he was the victim of a stacked decision by an intolerant court. From the colony's point of view he was a born troublemaker.

Whether Gorton was a troublemaker depends, of course, on the point of view. He had strong convictions about civil justice, which I shall return to. What he demanded in the way of religious freedom was the right to expound the mysteries of Christ as the spirit moved him, which meant in his case preaching a doctrine of mystical union between Christ and the regenerate, condemning all outward forms of worship, and reinterpreting the traditional teaching of the church on such matters as the Trinity or immortality to suit his fancy. He demanded a hearing for these opinions, which he considered were not his opinions but the Holy Ghost's; and, whenever he was whipped or banished, there was always some disciple standing by to cry, "Now Christ Jesus has suffered!" To molest him was certain to produce trouble, but what would happen if he ever found a place where he could enjoy the liberty he asked for?

The colony of Rhode Island eventually became such a place, with Gorton installed, after many adventures, as the founder of one of its four towns. The first of the separatist's three problems—the problem of persuading a community to make an experiment in soul liberty—was solved. This was due partly to the determination of prophets like Williams, Gorton, and Clark and partly to certain characteristics of these settlers which predisposed them to try such an experiment, the chief being the diversity of opinion among them which made an orthodoxy a practical impossibility, and the number of rebels against all clerical pretensions. The decision in favor of religious liberty was not made immediately by each community at the time of its migration; if Williams was committed to it when he founded Providence, the Antinomians were not committed to it when they founded Portsmouth and Newport. And after it became a rallying point for the common defense of the settlements against Massachusetts, there were plenty of second thoughts on the subject. There were elements, both in Providence and on the island, who would gladly have given up soul liberty for a little more social security and who were prepared either to submit themselves once again to Massachusetts or to carve out a more orthodox shelter for themselves. However, these elements were eventually defeated, and "soul liberty"—a liberty unique in the seventeenth century—became the distinguishing mark of Rhode Island.

The second problem for the separatist was to discover whether the emancipated religious conscience was capable of social discipline and, if so, what sort of discipline. What the religious separatist demanded was an area of freedom, "in matters of God's worship," within which, as he said, Christ was sole lord over the individual conscience. But how far did that area extend, and what human government was he prepared to obey outside that area? These were questions which separatists seldom faced while they were in opposition. They generally protested that they had no quarrel with the ordinary obligations of civil life, that all they wanted was their soul liberty, and that they would live gratefully under any government that gave it to them. But, as soul liberty came within reach, it soon became apparent that the questions would have to be faced and that no simple answer was going to be given to them.

If one surveys the history of separatists in different situations, one finds that their "soul liberty" can have at least four different consequences so far as the political order is concerned.

First, there is the possibility already mentioned—the separatist may become a militant millenarian. This happens only in revolutionary situations—of great hopes and great dangers—where saints are not quite sure whether they are going to be slaughtered or whether Christ is coming to rule the earth through them. This happened at Munster, and it happens in the English Revolution.

Second, "soul liberty" may lead to anarchism of one form or another. There is a story taken from the history of Antinomianism in England which describes the sort of people we are dealing with. It is told by a bitter enemy of the sects, but there is no reason to dismiss it as a freak of malicious fancy.

About the beginning of Lent last, Master Faucett, Minister of Walton upon the Thames in Surrey, preached in his parish church after dinner. When he came down out of his pulpit it was twilight; and into the church came six soldiers, one of them with a lantern in his hand and a candle burning in it; in the other hand he had four candles not lighted. He with the lantern called to the parishioners to stay a little, for he had a message to them from God; and offered to go up into the pulpit, but the parishioners would not let him; then he would have delivered his errand in the church, but there they would not hear him; so he went forth into the church-yard, the people following him; where he related to them:

That he had a vision and received a command from God to deliver his will unto them; which he was to deliver and they to receive upon pain of damnation. It consisted of five lights:

1. That the Sabbath was abolished as unnecessary, Jewish, and merely ceremonial. And here (quoth he) I should put out my first light, but the wind is so high I cannot light it.

2. Tythes are abolished as Jewish and ceremonial, a great burden to the Saints of God, and a discouragement of industry and tillage. And here I should put out my second light, etc., as aforesaid, which was the burden of his song.

3. Ministers are abolished as anti-Christian, and of no longer use now Christ himself descends into the hearts of his Saints, and his Spirit enlighteneth them with revelations, and inspirations. And here I should have to put out my third light, etc.

4. Magistrates are abolished as useless, now that Christ himself is in purity of spirit come amongst us, and hath erected the Kingdom of the Saints upon earth; and beside they are tyrants and oppressors of the Liberty of the Saints, and tie them to laws and ordinances, mere human inventions. And here I should have put out, etc.

5. Then putting his hand into his pocket, and pulling out a little Bible, he showed it open to the people, saying, "Here is a book you have in great veneration, consisting of two parts, the Old and New Testament; I must tell you, it is abolished: It containeth beggarly rudiments, milk for Babes. But now Christ is in Glory amongst us, and imparts a fuller measure of his Spirit to his Saints, than this can afford; and therefore I am commanded to burn it before your faces." So, taking the Candle out of his lantern, he set fire to the leaves. And then putting out the candle, cried, "And here my fifth light is extinguished."

This speaks for itself. The saint is capable of invoking his privileges to undermine all the obligations of social life. He may demand the right to sin in order to prove his superiority over sin. He will tell you that conduct which is sin in others is no sin in him. He may discover a conscientious objection to bearing office, paying taxes, or submitting to legal process. He may have suffered so much from authority that he thinks that society can get along without any. He will tell you that arbitration ought to replace government; that no law ought to be binding which is not approved by the individual conscience. This is a spirit which can be invoked to justify anything, and it results in conduct which ranges through different degrees of lawlessness from noncooperation in trifles to a complete repudiation of authority.

Third, the separatist may become a constitutionalist. He wants his "soul liberty," but, if he can get that, he is prepared to accept the English constitution as he finds it. Because of his experience of arbitrary power and his alliance with parliamentarians, he thinks of it as a liberal constitution. But it is not a democratic constitution, and he has no ambition to democratize it. He simply wants the securities for property, for personal liberty, and for representative government by the classes with a stake in the country, which are upheld by the English common-law tradition. Magna Carta, symbolizing a rule of law under a limited monarchy, is good enough for him. He is not interested in a Declaration of the Rights of Man.

Finally, the separatist may become a doctrinaire democrat. He demands that the state should be organized on the same principles as his little church. His religious congregation has a voluntary covenant as its basis; saints are regarded as equals; they settle their problems by free discussion. So, by analogy, the state ought to have a social contract as its basis; its citizens ought to be considered equal; and government ought to approximate to direct democracy as closely as possible.

Given this variety of possible inferences from the separatist position, it is not surprising that contemporaries equated them with anarchists and that Massachusetts and her associates spent thirty or forty years trying to wipe out Rhode Island. However, Rhode Island did demonstrate that its settlers were capable of enough social discipline to form a little commonwealth, which was able to defend itself against both internal disorder and external aggression. Of the four possible inferences of which I have spoken, it is agreed that Rhode Island was not plagued by millenarianism of the violent variety. There is the millenarianism of the frustrated prophet who may feel in his own mind that the world is so wicked that God is bound to be coming to judge it soon; but there is no party with swords in their hands trying to seize power. That is a mood which thrives on persecution and which assails the saint when he is backed into a corner. But here it was always possible for Samuel Gorton to obey the apostolic injunction, "If they persecute you in one city, flee into another." And when he had exhausted them all, he could build his own.

It has been suggested that the fourth line of development did occur—the line which turns the separatist into an advocate of the rights of man. And Roger Williams, in particular, has been hailed as the "Irrepressible Democrat": a champion of social democracy who gave the best efforts of his later years to the construction of a democratic republic and who fought a noble, losing struggle against the encroaching forces of colonial privilege. But this is based on a misreading of his character and his writings. He was irrepressible enough, and noble enough, but it is the irrepressibility and the nobility of the passionate pilgrim who spends his life trying to save souls and to win for them the soul liberty they desire. He would have taken soul liberty gratefully from any government. He is content to enjoy it in Rhode Island either under the authority of Parliament, a Cromwellian dictatorship, or a restored Stuart. When he visits England in the course of the Revolution, it is the struggle for soul liberty that interests him, not the struggle for civil liberty. He has no contacts with the Levellers, the only genuinely democratic party thrown up by Puritanism. When he has to concern himself in Rhode Island with the details of political organization—a task for which he had no particular talent—he shows himself to be a constitutionalist, trying to adapt English representative institutions to a frontier situation, but with no commitment to social democracy. The passages in his writings which are usually quoted as evidence of a faith in political equality turn out to be either a separatist's protest against clerical privilege or simply a Christian protest against greed.

What Rhode Island actually experiences, in terms of my four alternatives, is the miscellaneous lawlessness of the second category which is gradually surmounted by the constitutionalism of the third. The result is a commonwealth which bears the marks of its original individualism for the next hundred years, in various habits of noncooperation and obstructionism, but which offers no resistance to the emergence of a little colonial aristocracy built out of fortunes in land and trade and concentrating effective power in its own hands. William Coddington, one of these little aristocrats, spent years of his life trying to avoid having to live under the same government as Samuel Gorton, even if it meant taking the island back under the wing of Massachusetts or getting authority from England to govern it himself. But he might have spared himself the worry. Once Gorton had complete freedom to prophesy in a town of his own making and the privilege of being a magistrate under a constitution sanctioned by English authority and observing English common-law principles—he was always a great stickler for that—he gave no further trouble. Though the prophet continued to be a prophet, the born nuisance disappeared.

What of the last of the separatist's problems—the one he shares with all Puritans? Could he succeed, any better than they, in keeping the crusading energy alive?

However we may judge the experiment in Rhode Island, it is clear that a Williams or a Gorton would judge it by the progress of conversions, by the appearance of more and more prophets, and by the conviction that this haven for the persecuted would form a beacon for the whole world. Before he died in 1683, after one of the most strenuous and impetuous Puritan pilgrimages on record, Roger Williams had his own reasons for frustration. He had fought a lifelong battle with the proprietors of Providence to preserve that town as a public trust for religious refugees, only to see it turned into an investment company for the founding families. That defeat became a symbol of the future. In 1664 he wrote a letter to Winthrop's son: "Sir, when we that have been the eldest and are rotting [in our graves] a generation will act, I fear, far unlike the first Winthrops and their *Models of Christian Charity:* I fear that the common trinity of the world—Profit, Preferment, Pleasure—will be here the *tria omnia,* as in all the world besides: that Prelacy and Popery too will in this wilderness predominate; and that God Land will be as great a God with us English as God Gold was with the Spaniard."

There were no more Puritan prophets to follow Williams and Gorton. Gorton left a few Gortonists behind him, but a sect which subsists on a personality is not going to last long. His theology is unintelligible. A disciple of Vane, another Puritan mystic who left a few Vanists behind him, said of his master, "He was a partaker of the Divine Nature (2 Pet. 1.4), 'tis past the skill of humane nature to interpret him. . . . He had the *New Name,* which no man knowes but he that hath it." The last disciple of Samuel Gorton sufficiently explained the disappearance of Gortonism when he said that his books "were written in Heaven, and no one could read and understand them unless he was in Heaven."

Admittedly another race of prophets

were to reap where the seekers and mystics had sowed. A community which stood fast by religious liberty, and which still contained many enthusiasts within its otherwise secularized membership, was ready to receive Quakerism. But Quakerism, the last eruption of spiritual lava from the seventeenth-century volcano, goes through the same cooling process of compromise and concession as Puritanism, and we may infer from the fact that William Coddington embraced it that its adaptation to the habits of prudent businessmen in the rising town of Newport was fairly swift. The Rhode Island which enters the eighteenth century has many sterling qualities, but from the point of view of its utopian founders it is a shell which has lost its kernel.

Suggestions for Additional Reading

No single selection of readings can do full justice to the complexities and to the enduring significance of this subject. Any inquisitive reader will find much of value remaining in the original works from which excerpts have been reprinted here. The full range of Roger Williams's thought is best seen in *The Writings of Roger Williams,* six volumes published by the Narragansett Club (Providence, 1866–1874), which also includes John Cotton's side of the debate. Perry Miller has made more easily available and readable much of the best of Williams's writings in Miller, *Roger Williams: His Contribution to the American Tradition* (New York, 1953), soon to be available in paperback. The evidence on which Dexter bases his defense of the Massachusetts authorities is fully spelled out in Henry M. Dexter, *As to Roger Williams* (Boston, 1876). Alan Simpson, *Puritanism in Old and New England* (Chicago, 1955) also provides brief and penetrating chapters on the essential nature of Puritanism and its expression in the Bible Commonwealth of Massachusetts Bay.

The most recent biography of Williams, a brief and judicious one, is Ola Winslow, *Master Roger Williams* (New York, 1957). Earlier biographies like Edward J. Carpenter, *Roger Williams* (New York, 1909), and James E. Ernst, *Roger Williams* (New York, 1932), largely parallel, with less detail, the interpretation presented here by Brockunier. This emphasis on Williams as essentially a democratic political philosopher is spelled out by James E. Ernst, *The Political Thought of Roger Williams* (Seattle, 1929). The recent sharp repudiation of this view of Williams was profoundly influenced by one key article which helped to make clear what Williams shared with the Massachusetts Puritans: Mauro Calamandrei, "Neglected Aspects of Roger Williams' Thought," *Church History,* XXI (September, 1952), 239–259.

Numerous efforts have been made to explain the differences between Williams and Massachusetts: G. A. Stead, "Roger Williams and the Massachusetts-Bay," *New England Quarterly,* VII (1934), 235–257; R. E. E. Harkness, "Roger Williams —Prophet of Tomorrow," *Journal of Religion,* XV (1935), 400–425; H. B. Parkes, "John Cotton and Roger Williams Debate Toleration," *New England Quarterly,* IV (1931), 735–756. Somewhat more sympathetic than others to Cotton's position is Elizabeth F. Hirsch, "John Cotton and Roger Williams," *Church History,* X (1941), 38–51. A balanced appraisal from the viewpoint of a political scientist is Clinton Rossiter, *Seedtime of the Republic* (New York, 1953), Chapter 7.

The body of writings on the whole question of religious liberty is, of course, voluminous. A. P. Stokes, *Church and State in the United States* (New York, 1950) is a comprehensive study in three volumes. Much briefer and in many ways more relevant and pointed for understanding the role of Roger Williams is Evarts B. Greene, *Religion and the State* (New York, 1941). A succinct and informed treatment of the relations between Puritanism and religious liberty appears in William Haller, "The Puritan Background of the First Amendment" in Conyers Read, ed., *The Constitution Reconsidered* (New York, 1938), 131–141. Finally, any reader wishing to understand the religious reasons for separation of church and state should look at the argument presented in Winthrop Hudson, *The Great Tradition of the American Churches* (New York, 1953), especially chapters 1–3 and 11. Professor Hudson here draws upon the whole historical tradition of religious liberty in America as a necessary element in revitalizing the American churches. In many ways his book restates fundamental concerns of Roger Williams and makes them relevant to the present state of religion in our country.